BOOK 2

ENGLISH IN CONTEXT

Reading Comprehension
for Science and Technology

Joan M. Saslow

John F. Mongillo

Prentice-Hall, Inc., Englewood Cliffs, New Jersey   07632

62471

Library of Congress Cataloging in Publication Data
(Revised for volume 2)

APR 0 7 1985

Saslow, Joan M.   (date)
    English in context.

    1. English language—Text-books for foreign speakers.
2. English language—Technical English.   3. College
readers.   4. Readers—Science.   5. Readers—Technology.
I. Mongillo, John F.   II. Title.
PE1128.S274   1985   428.6'4'0245   84-4800
ISBN   0-13-280025-X (v. 1)

Editorial/production supervision and
        interior design: Barbara Alexander
Cover design: Whitman Studio, Inc.
Photo research: Teri Stratford
Manufacturing buyer: Harry P. Baisley

Cover photo credit: Courtesy NASA
Lesson opening photo credits:

1: Courtesy General Electric; 2: Courtesy General Motors; 3: © Lewis Walker from
National Audubon Society, Photo Researchers, Inc.; 4: Shirley Richards, Photo
Researchers, Inc.; 5: American Red Cross; 6: Lowell Observatory; 7: Motor
Vehicle Manufacturers Association of the United States, Inc.; 8: United Nations
Photo by M. Tzovaras; 9: USDA Photo; 10: U.S. Air Force Photo

Printed in the United States of America

10   9   8   7   6   5   4   3   2   1

ISBN 0-13-280033-0   01

PRENTICE-HALL INTERNATIONAL, INC., *London*
PRENTICE-HALL OF AUSTRALIA PTY. LIMITED, *Sydney*
EDITORA PRENTICE-HALL DO BRASIL, LTDA., *Rio de Janeiro*
PRENTICE-HALL OF CANADA, LTD., *Toronto*
PRENTICE-HALL OF INDIA PRIVATE LIMITED, *New Delhi*
PRENTICE-HALL OF JAPAN, INC., *Tokyo*
PRENTICE-HALL OF SOUTHEAST ASIA PTE. LTD., *Singapore*
WHITEHALL BOOKS LIMITED, *Wellington, New Zealand*

Contents

Preface

Purpose

English in Context: Reading Comprehension for Science and Technology is an intermediate-level reading comprehension text series for people who want concentrated practice in reading scientific and technical English. The only purpose of this three-level text series is to build the comprehension skill. Although it is unarguably true that listening, speaking, and writing enhance the reading skill, practice in reading itself is a more direct route to this goal. To this end *English in Context: Reading Comprehension for Science and Technology* elicits no production of written or spoken English, and includes no listening comprehension activities. Students at the intermediate level have already been exposed to years of classroom practice of "the four skills." What is provided here, then, is an alternate path focused entirely on reading.

Student Profile

English in Context: Reading Comprehension for Science and Technology, Book 2, is intended either for students who have successfully completed Book 1 of the series, or who know the meaning of 80 percent of the active vocabulary words from Book 1 and can read the first reading selection in Book 2 with 75 percent comprehension, as measured by Exercise C on page 14. Although students ready to begin Book 2 are more proficient in their ability to read scientific and technical prose than students at the Book 1 level are, these students will still encounter great difficulty in reading primary materials found in college-level textbooks, technical manuals, and professional journals.

It should be kept in mind that the students for whom these three texts in the *English in Context* series were created are not English majors, but rather are specialists (or specialists in training) in some area of science or technology.

Scope of the Series

The series in general in intended for students who have had beginning-level courses in English, either at the secondary-school level or at the university, the technical school, or the binational institute. These students typically have had two- to three-hundred hours of classroom instruction, often in large classes. They have been exposed, at one time or another (and with greater or lesser amounts of success), to the "basic structures" of the language, and have a fair vocabulary covering everyday activities, work, school, play, and hobbies. They function conversationally at a low level and make many mistakes in grammar, lexicon, and pronunciation. They understand more difficult language than that which they can produce on their own. Their reading ability generally corresponds to what they can say, because they have studied from texts that "strictly control" the reading narratives. These students approach all unfamiliar readings with a bilingual dictionary close at hand, since they are unskilled in deriving meaning from passages containing new words without translating every new word into their own language. They are particularly handicapped when facing a scientific or technical reading because their training has been in "everyday" English.

English in Context: Reading Comprehension for Science and Technology Books 1 and 2 are similar in design and format, while Book 3 differs significantly. Since the purpose of the series as a whole is to prepare students to read authentic published source materials in any area of science or technology, the first two books concentrate on reading selections especially written to ready students for this goal by illustrating the use of high-frequency science vocabulary and important concepts in grammar and syntax. Book 3, on the other hand, has been designed to bridge the gap between the "engineered" reading selections of Books 1 and 2 and free reading, in that it centers on real, unedited excerpts from published science textbooks and journals while maintaining a good deal of supporting exercise and explanatory material.

Working Assumptions

Underlying the development of these materials are several assumptions. The first is that scientific and technical English are English. The characteristic features of this type of writing are all found in all other forms of English. Colin R. Elliot has remarked that [except for technical terms and some more complex structures] "there is little to distinguish it from any other form of writing which seeks to explain and exemplify general theories or describe processes" (ELT Journal, October 1976). J.D. Corbluth (ELT Journal, July 1975) even disagrees that there is such a thing as scientific English at all. Although other possible grammatical frameworks exist (notably Ewer's Microacts, for example), we have chosen to base these materials on the assumption that the similarities between scientific/technical English and ordinary English are greater than the differences between them, always recognizing, however, that students predictably will have difficulty with certain syntactical and grammatical features which occur frequently. Some well-recognized examples of these are passive voice, noun compounds, *if*-clauses, long pre-posed modifying clusters, and reduced adjective clauses. These have been given particular emphasis.

In addition to the choice of the syntactical and grammatical features in each lesson, certain words were chosen for inclusion in the vocabulary sections at the beginning of each lesson. It is our working assumption that most of these words are probably not known by the student who has had the two- to three-hundred hours of English described above. These words are found over and over in scientific and technical prose. Most of them are of a type we call "subtechnical," that is, they are not highly specialized for one narrow field of interest, but rather are found in writings in all areas of science and technology. It is our belief that knowing these words will greatly increase comprehension of scientific and technical narrative. These words are further and more specifically described below under Vocabulary.

"Vocabulary of ideas" is another category of words included in the Vocabulary section at the beginning of each lesson. These words are not really "science" or "technology" words at all but rather are used frequently to express concepts and ideas in the type of writing students will be reading. It must be admitted, however, that the inclusion of some words under one or the other rubric is sometimes debatable and concededly made on a subjective, and sometimes almost arbitrary, basis. The major value of having the vocabulary divided into two parts is to "lighten the load" of words to be be learned at one time. We chose to distinguish these two gross categories of words in the belief that some of the vocabulary, though not at all "scientific" or "technical" (such as *predominantly*) are used with extremely high frequency in scientific and technical prose. Furthermore, we felt that these words differ in a general way from more strictly "scientific" or "technical" words, such as, for example, *buoyancy*. Although this distinction is very clear for these two examples, we must recognize that the choice of placement for all words is not always that evident.

Organization and Lesson Format

Each lesson in *English in Context: Reading Comprehension for Science and Technology* is built around a reading selection on a timely scientific or technical topic. *All other sections of the lesson are tightly connected to the reading, either as a preparation for it or an extension of it.* In this way, every word and every exercise deals with comprehension of the central reading selection of the lesson.

VOCABULARY*

The vocabulary section that appears at the beginning of each lesson is made up of Sub-technical Vocabulary, Vocabulary of Ideas, and, occasionally, Thought Connectors. Each lesson presents twenty to thirty important new words.

*Note: *All* vocabulary in this section is used in the reading selection appearing later in the lesson.

Subtechnical Vocabulary. Some examples are *stationary, surroundings, homogeneous, exploitation, gear, sample, to last, to exert, norm, intake, modality, to induce, to arise,* and *variable.* Almost all these words will be found sooner or later in students' independent reading, regardless of their specialized interests. Each word is defined in the limited sense in which it is used in the reading selection to follow. The word is then presented in a simple contextual sentence which further conveys and fixes its meaning. Where necessary or helpful, an illustration is also provided as a meaning conveyor.

Vocabulary of Ideas. These words and expressions are also taken from the reading selection to follow and are less technical *per se* than the words described above. (For the rationale for the division between "subtechnical vocabulary" and "vocabulary of ideas" see Working Assumptions, above.) Some examples of such words are *to rule out, to assume, to give rise to, to guard against, materially, to keep pace with, at the outset, as evidenced by,* and *fully.* As with the Subtechnical Vocabulary, each word is defined and used in a contextual sentence.

Thought Connectors. When included, these rhetorical items are essential connectors of ideas in scientific and technical writing. Some examples are *conversely, regardless,* and *in spite of the fact that.*

Vocabulary Exercises. If learners remembered words after seeing them only once, then these exercises would not be necessary. It is every language teacher's experience that in order to make vocabulary "active," rigorous practice is necessary. All too often at the intermediate level, students' vocabularies stop growing because it is assumed that practice is only appropriate for beginners. A series of exercises in each of these lessons provides students with yet another opportunity to see each of the vocabulary words from that lesson in a relevant contextual sentence. These exercises are not a test. They are meant to help commit meaning to memory. Not only will each word be elicited as an answer to a question, but it also will be used several other times in items eliciting other vocabulary words as answers.

COMPREHENSION SKILL INDEX (Skills and Syntactical/Grammatical Concepts)

Before and after the reading selection in each lesson, facsimiles of index cards signal the names of comprehension skills or important grammatical or syntactical concepts presented in that lesson. These skills and topics comprise the comprehension index. Some of the skills are: skimming, scanning, reading comprehension, confirming content, understanding vocabulary from context, understanding vocabulary from word parts, distinguishing fact from opinion, reference, and drawing conclusions. Syntactical and grammatical topics include adjective clauses, noun clauses, long preposed modifying clusters, and uncommon word order. Throughout, great care has been taken in deciding the teaching approach necessary when the goal is comprehension and not production of the various syntactical and grammatical concepts. In addition, students do intensive work with the reading selection in that lesson, making sure they can comprehend the grammatical or syntactical concept at hand. The reading selection has, in fact, been written specifically to use the targeted syntax or grammar concept numerous times. In Lesson four, for example, long preposed modifying clusters are presented. The reading selection in that lesson contains no fewer than thirty of these clusters.

Comprehension Index Exercises. In each section of the comprehension index, exercises are provided. It is important to note that no production of the targeted concepts is necessary in these exercises. Rather, students receive practice in deriving meaning from sentences containing the targeted concepts. All sentences used in these exercises come from the reading selection, providing cross reinforcement of each concept.

READING SELECTION

The reading selection is the core of each lesson and the source of all the vocabulary, comprehension index skills, and syntax and grammar topics presented in that lesson. Each reading concerns an exciting subject designed to be of interest to any modern reader who has a basic knowledge of science and who lives in today's world. A glance at the titles of these selections in the Table of Contents will make this apparent. Care has also been taken in ensuring that the instructor with a humanities rather than a science background will be comfortable teaching these selections.

The readings get linguistically more complex, conceptually denser, and rhetorically more sophisticated as each book develops. As previously pointed out, each reading uses numerous examples of the syntactical and grammatical concepts targeted in that lesson. In addition, each of the vocabulary words that appeared in the vocabulary section at the beginning of the lesson appears at least once in the reading selection. These vocabulary words can be easily spotted, as they appear in boldface type, reminding the student to notice these important words once more in the context of the reading selection.

The side notes that appear alongside the reading define words that most students probably do not know. These words are less essential for a student's active vocabulary because of their lower frequency in scientific and technical writing. However, some of these words should be considered active vocabulary by specialists in the particular field dealt with in the reading. An example of such a word is *thyrotoxicosis* in Lesson 5. Any student whose main interest is medicine—or particularly internal medicine or endocrinology—will find this to be an important word. Most other students will not; for this reason, *thyrotoxicosis* was not included in the Subtechnical Vocabulary at the beginning of the lesson but instead is side noted alongside its occurrence in the reading.

JOAN M. SASLOW

JOHN F. MONGILLO

LESSON ONE

Medical Diagnosis Through Nuclear Magnetic Resonance Imaging

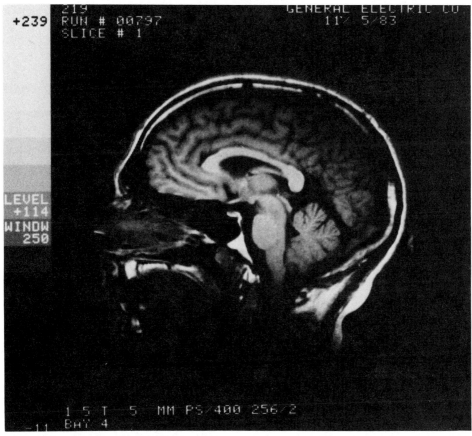

A view of the head on an NMR

Subtechnical Vocabulary

noninvasive (adjective)

> nonsurgical; not entering the body

> X-rays are a **noninvasive** device for viewing the interior of the body.

longitudinal (adjective)

> along the length of the body, or of an organ

> A complete **longitudinal** view of a tree would show the tree from the top to the bottom.

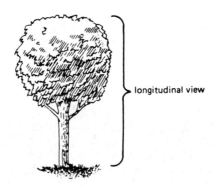

longitudinal view

diagnosis (noun)

> discovery or identification of a patient's disease

> **Diagnosis** of a disease is usually necessary before treatment can begin.

tissue (noun)

> a group of similar cells attached to one another

> Organs are made up of **tissues**.

infertility (noun)

> inability to produce offspring

> Many causes for **infertility** can now be diagnosed and treated.

malignancy (noun)

> cancer; cancerous tumor

> The diagnosis of a **malignancy** is very alarming to both the patient and the doctor.

cross section (noun)

> surface or plane created by a cut through an object, body, or organ, used for study
>
> A **cross section** of a carrot is round.

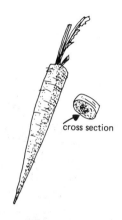

cross section

carcinogenesis (noun)

> the process of causing cancer
>
> It is known that cigarettes are an important factor in **carcinogenesis**.

sheath (noun)

> a close covering for a long object, open at one or both ends
>
> A **sheath** is often used to protect a knife.

sheath

site (noun)

> place; locus
>
> Uranium has been discovered at several **sites** near here.

target (noun)

> object to be shot at or reached with another object; goal
>
> The **target** of chemotherapy is often a tumor.

target

progress (noun)

> advancement; scientific or technological developmental activity
>
> In disease control much **progress** has resulted from the development of antibiotics.

side effects (noun)

> unwanted effects from a medicine
>
> A **side effect** of aspirin is bleeding.

to employ (verb)

> to use
>
> Radiation **is** often **employed** in cancer treatment.

to revert (verb)

> to return to a former position or condition
>
> Environmentalists hope that if industrial pollution is reduced, acid rain will stop, and fish populations **will revert** to their former numbers.

to behave (verb)

> to act
>
> Cancer cells **behave** differently from normal cells.

to inject (verb)

>   to put into the body through the use of a hollow needle

>   Penicillin **can** either **be injected** or taken by mouth.

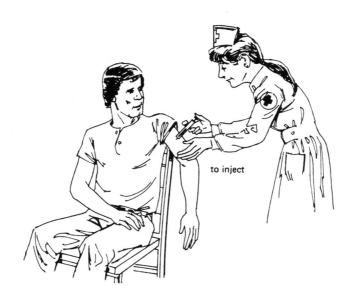

to inject

to assess (verb)

>   to evaluate; to measure effectiveness

>   It is difficult **to assess** the financial impact of acid rain.

to probe (verb)

>   to examine, generally by touching or entering with an instrument

>   Dentists **probe** the teeth to look for cavities.

to facilitate (verb)

>   to make easier or more efficient; to aid

>   Retina reattachment **has been facilitated** by the new laser technology.

to wear away (phrasal verb)

>   to be consumed with use

>   The more friction there is, the sooner the material **will wear away**.

Vocabulary of Ideas

means (noun)

> way of doing something; a method for reaching a goal
>
> Doctors are looking for a harmless **means** of observing the interior of the body.

anomaly (noun)

> abnormality or irregularity, usually in form
>
> The patient was born with an **anomaly** in one ear, and has never been able to hear with that ear.

actually (adverb)

> in reality; really
>
> A stroke can **actually** be caused by a severe buildup in arterial plaque.

paradoxically (adverb)

> in the exact opposite way one would expect; contrary to what one would expect
>
> **Paradoxically**, cancer treatment itself can be carcinogenic if it is poorly administered.

essentially (adverb)

> approximately; almost; for the most part
>
> Most doctors give **essentially** the same advice for the treatment of a cold: bed rest, aspirin, and fluids.

instrumental (adjective)

> causative
>
> She has been **instrumental** in getting the others to see that their research methods are not effective.

in essence

> on the whole; essentially
>
> **In essence**, there is not much that can be done to prevent a cold.

in question

> the specific thing or idea being considered
>
> The organ **in question** in today's anatomy lesson is the heart.

Vocabulary Exercises

A. Complete the following sentences with words from the list.

side effects	means
progress	in essence
diagnosis	target
facilitate	revert
actually	assess

1. The term *heart disease* includes, _____, anything that goes wrong with the heart or the circulatory system.

2. Even though aspirin is a nonprescription medicine, _____ it is the best medicine for many serious conditions.

3. It is hoped that using an alternate element in photovoltaic cells will _____ their wider use as an energy supplier.

4. Staphylococcus is the _____ of several antibiotics.

5. After successful radiation treatment, many tumors _____ to a smaller size, giving the patient more time to live a healthy life.

6. An X-ray of the teeth is one _____ of detecting decay that cannot be observed simply by looking in the patient's mouth.

7. Unfortunately, the most effective drugs often are the ones that have the largest number of _____.

8. After treatment of a disease or a condition, it is important to _____ the effectiveness of that treatment.

9. Very little _____ has been made in the prevention of acid rain.

10. A _____ of cancer no longer necessarily means a shortened life.

B. Choose the correct lettered response to complete each numbered statement.

1. Some medicines are _____ into a muscle, while others must be taken intravenously.
   a. probed
   b. injected
   c. facilitated
   d. reverted

2. Sometimes, _____, the best physicians are not the ones who had the highest grades in medical school.
   a. longitudinally
   b. in question
   c. in essence
   d. paradoxically

3. Abnormal cells that grow very fast are a _____.
   a. diagnosis
   b. malignancy
   c. tissue
   d. sheath

4. The _____ of a malignancy often determines its seriousness.
   a. target
   b. cross section
   c. site
   d. diagnosis

5. _____ diagnostic methods are less likely to have side effects and complications than surgical ones.
   a. Noninvasive
   b. Longitudinal
   c. In essence
   d. Actually

6. The only way to know if a tumor is malignant or not is to take a biopsy of the tumor

   _____ and study its cells under the microscope.
   a. malignancy
   b. in question
   c. in essence
   d. progress

7. Many industrial chemicals are suspected of _____.
   a. carcinogenesis
   b. side effects
   c. diagnosis
   d. progress

8. It is well known that _____ may result from the too frequent use of X-rays.
   a. progress
   b. targets
   c. tissues
   d. infertility

9. Although all sharks are generally feared, it is not true that all sharks _____ in the same way.
   a. wear away
   b. revert

c. behave

d. facilitate

10. A(n) _____ of a tissue can be studied under the microscope.
    a. sheath
    b. cross section
    c. anomaly
    d. carcinogenesis

11. A(n) _____ is sometimes harmless and sometimes harmful.
    a. anomaly
    b. infertility
    c. cross section
    d. target

12. Vaccination of the majority of children has been _____ in the elimination of several serious diseases.
    a. in essence
    b. noninvasive
    c. longitudinal
    d. instrumental

13. Synthetic and natural vitamins are _____ the same.
    a. paradoxically
    b. essentially
    c. longitudinally
    d. anomaly

14. A _____ covers something, usually in order to protect it.
    a. sheath
    b. diagnosis
    c. target
    d. means

15. Cotton is easier to _____ than steel is.
    a. wear away
    b. revert
    c. behave
    d. facilitate

16. A _____ section differs from a cross section in that it presents a surface of the whole length of the object in question.
    a. noninvasive
    b. instrumental
    c. longitudinal
    d. malignant

17. Many pointed instruments are _____ in the practice of dentistry.
    a. employed
    b. facilitated

c. reverted

d. instrumental

18. The skin is a _____ that covers the body.

    a. target

    b. malignancy

    c. sheath

    d. tissue

19. In order to vaporize plaque with a burst of laser light, it is necessary to _____ the artery with a fiber glass tube.

    a. probe

    b. facilitate

    c. employ

    d. wear away

Understanding Vocabulary from Word Parts

Suffixes

Suffixes are grouped in two classes. Class 1 suffixes change the number, person, or tense of a word (books, sees, typed). Class 2 suffixes are used to change the part of speech of a word, for example, from a noun to a verb or from an adjective to a verb, and so on.

The following class 2 suffixes form verbs.

-ate (changes nouns or adjectives to verbs)

Noun or Adjective	Verb
active	activate
capacity	capacitate
facility	facilitate
origin	originate
radius	radiate

-en (changes adjectives or nouns to verbs)

Adjective or Noun	Verb
dead	deaden
deep	deepen
red	redden
white	whiten
height	heighten
strength	strengthen

-ify (changes nouns and adjectives to verbs)

Noun or Adjective	Verb
class	classify
electric	electrify
pure	purify

-ize (changes nouns and adjectives to verbs)—*ise* in British English

Noun or Adjective	Verb
atom	atomize
computer	computerize
crystal	crystallize
hospital	hospitalize
magnet	magnetize
rubber	rubberize
standard	standardize
sterile	sterilize

A patient about to undergo testing in the Signa investigational high-field superconducting magnetic resonance scanning system

Courtesy General Electric

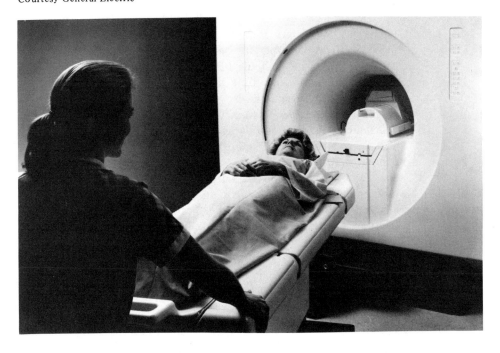

Medical Diagnosis Through Nuclear Magnetic Resonance Imaging

For years doctors have been looking for **noninvasive means** to observe the interior of the human body for **diagnosis** of abnormalities of **tissues**, bones, and organs. Although X-rays, which have been in use since 1895, show bones clearly, soft tissues appear fuzzy on the X-ray screen. X-rays therefore have limited value in soft-tissue observation. In recent years much **progress** has occurred and a few new diagnostic tools which **facilitate** interior anatomical observation of soft tissue have emerged. These diagnostic tools, called scanners, can produce computer-made pictures of **cross sections** of a patient's body. One scanner, called the CAT (Computerized Axial Tomography), is **actually** an X-ray machine linked to a computer. This machine allows doctors to study cross-sectional views of the head and body. Another kind, known as the PET (Positron Emission Computed Tomography) scanner, **employs** radioactive isotopes. These isotopes **are injected** into the body in order to detect certain chemical reactions within the body, particularly ones which occur in the brain. Both scanners are highly useful in diagnosing **malignancies, anomalies**, and diseases. They are, however, potentially dangerous, because they make use of the ionizing radiation of X-rays, which in large doses can damage cells and cause **infertility**. In addition, they may—**paradoxically**—be **instrumental** in **carcinogenesis**.

1

Many medical technologists believe that the ideal scanner is the newest one, known as the Nuclear Magnetic Resonance Scanner, or NMR. This scanner performs **essentially** the same diagnostic role as the CAT scanner and the PET scanner. But unlike these two scanners, the NMR doesn't use X-rays or radiation. Instead, it uses radio waves and magnetism.

2

myelin: white fatty material

Medical technologists can use the NMR to observe processes which are taking place in the tissues and organs. One process it can observe is blood flowing through an artery. The NMR can reveal damage from a stroke beneath the skull, diagnose spinal disk problems, and **assess** arthritis treatment. In addition, NMR scans are used on patients suffering from multiple sclerosis, which is known as MS. In this disease the fatty myelin **sheaths** that surround the nerve fibers **are worn away** and replaced with hard plaques at multiple **sites** along their length. The NMR has an advantage over the other scanners in diagnosing MS and in monitoring treatment success because it can detect more plaques than other scanners. This is possible because unlike other scanners, which can only observe cross sections of tissues and organs, the NMR is capable of viewing **longitudinal**

3

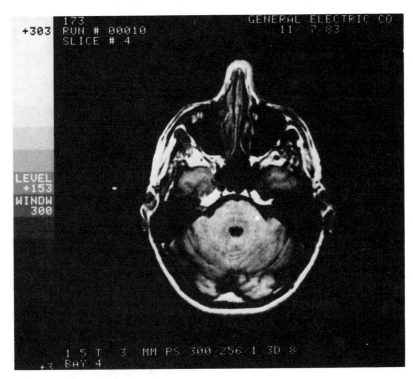

Image of the head on an NMR
Courtesy of General Electric

sections of the patient's body. Because of this capability, the NMR may even be used in observing plaque buildup in the coronary arteries.

Modus Operandi

In performing an **NMR** scan, the technician places the patient on a table inside the chute of a large, doughnut-shaped magnet. The NMR magnetic force is so strong that it affects certain atomic nuclei in the cells, tissues, and organs of the human body. The magnetic field causes the nuclei of certain atoms to align themselves with the direction of the field. **In essence**, the nuclei themselves **behave** as tiny magnets. To produce an image, the NMR emits a radio signal that creates a second, or alternating, magnetic force at right angles to the first field. When the radio signal is turned off, the nuclei **revert** to their original position, emitting an electromagnetic signal. A computer analyzes the signal and reconstructs it to form a vivid image of the **target** tissue or organ. The image not only shows the location and size of the tissue or organ **in question** but indicates its

align: get in a straight line

vivid: clear and bright

4

composition and contents as well. Healthy and diseased tissues and organs produce different NMR images.

Application

Presently there are only a few **NMR** scanners built and available. Most hospitals are using the **CAT** or the **PET**. However, the future looks promising for the **NMR**. Many medical centers and hospitals currently have **NMR** scanners on order. Although the **NMR** may cost more than U.S. $1.5 million each, many medical technologists believe that this is the only scanner that will enable them to do noninvasive internal **probing** to see processes of life which have never before been seen—and to do this safely, without adverse **side effects**.

on order: bought but not yet received

5

Comprehension

EXERCISE

C. Insert **one** word taken directly from the reading to complete the following statements.

1. Doctors have been searching for a nonsurgical _____ of interior anatomical observation.

2. They find it important to observe the inside of the body in order to identify

   _____ and diseases.

3. Doctors have used _____ for almost one hundred years.

4. One disadvantage of X-rays is the _____ appearance of soft tissues on the screen.

5. Recently some new _____ have made diagnosis easier.

6. These tools are known as _____ .

7. The _____ scanner presents an X-ray cross section of a body part.

8. Scanners are instrumental in the diagnosis of _____ and other diseases.

9. The scanners are potentially dangerous because _____ , in large doses, are probably carcinogenic.

10. Many people consider the **NMR** to be _____ .

11. Although the **NMR** is very different from the **CAT** and the **PET**, it carries out

    _____ the same task as they do.

12. Instead of X-rays and radiation, the **NMR** relies on radio waves and

    _____ .

13. Arterial blood flow is a _____ the NMR can observe.

14. An NMR scan can permit doctors to view _____ damage without physically entering the skull.

15. An NMR scan can also help doctors evaluate the treatment of

    _____.

16. An acronym for multiple sclerosis is _____.

17. In MS hard plaques replace the myelin sheaths along _____ fibers.

18. Other scanners cannot view _____ sections like the NMR can.

19. Through use of the NMR, it may even be possible to see the interior of arteries for

    _____ buildup observation.

20. For an NMR scan, the patient lies inside a round _____.

21. Cell nuclei are affected by the _____ magnetic force.

22. The nuclei act on the whole the way _____ do.

23. After the radio signal is turned off, the nuclei go back to their original

    _____.

24. During this process the nuclei emit an electromagnetic _____.

25. The computerized _____ shows the location, size, composition, and contents of the target tissue or organ.

26. From this "picture," observers can assess whether the organ is diseased or

    _____.

27. The NMR is the only noninvasive internal observation device that permits safe

    probing with no _____ effects.

Vocabulary in Context

EXERCISE

D. Choose the correct lettered response to define each numbered term.

  1. imaging (title)
     a. picturing
     b. thinking about
  2. fuzzy (¶ 1)
     a. not clear
     b. bonelike

3. ideal (¶ 2)
   a. imaginary
   b. best

4. *modus operandi* (¶ 4 subhead)
   a. the way it works
   b. surgical operation

5. chute (¶ 4)
   a. box
   b. center hole

6. at right angles to (¶ 4)
   a. correctly
   b. perpendicular to

7. adverse (¶ 5)
   a. bad
   b. good

Drawing Conclusions

EXERCISE

E. Choose a or b to answer each question.

1. Why do doctors prefer noninvasive means of observing the inside of the body?
   a. because the alternative, surgery, carries the risk of complications
   b. because they are more accurate than the NMR

2. Why are X-rays the means of choice in the diagnosis of broken bones?
   a. because they cannot show soft tissues
   b. because they show bones clearly

3. Which diagnostic means would show a better picture of the brain?
   a. a CAT scan
   b. a conventional X-ray

4. Why is the NMR scanner safer and less likely to cause cancer than the CAT scanner or the PET scanner?
   a. because it doesn't use X-rays or radioactive isotopes
   b. because it can observe soft tissues better

5. Why can the NMR observe more plaques than the other scanners in patients with MS?
   a. because it can see a cross section of their coronary arteries
   b. because it can see the whole length of a nerve fiber

6. In what way do the cell nuclei behave like magnets?
   a. They stick to one another.
   b. They respond to the changing polarity of the magnetic field by moving.

7. Why do the nuclei revert to their original position when the radio signal is turned off?
   a. because they are no longer affected by the magnetic field
   b. because they emit an electromagnetic signal

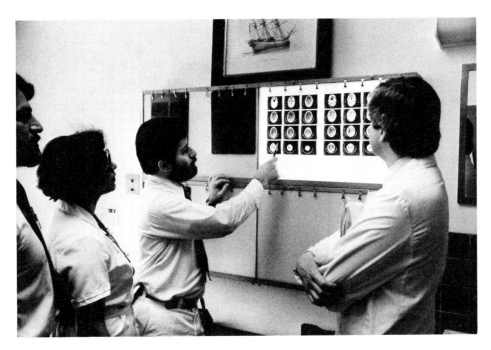

Doctors checking images made by a CAT scanner
Ken Karp

Relative Clauses (Adjective Clauses) Introduced by *That* or *Which* as Subjects of the Clause

Identifying Antecedents

A relative clause, also known as an adjective clause, modifies a noun (and some pronouns) that appears earlier in the same sentence.

examples: The sulfur *that enters the atmosphere today* will be tomorrow's acid rain.

     Sharks, *which are among the most ancient sea animals,* have a very bad reputation.

     The most promising of the new hybrids is amaranth, *which can grow in almost any kind of soil.*

The noun or pronoun modified by the adjective (or relative) clause is called the antecedent. Being able to identify the antecedent is essential for comprehension.

examples: The book *which contains all the statistics about sulfur emissions* is no longer in the library. (antecedent: book)

Everything *that happens* during an operation is important. (antecedent: everything)

Some safe medicines are available for conditions *which occur during pregnancy.* (antecedent: conditions)

Relative Clauses (Adjective Clauses) Introduced by That *or* Which *as Subjects of the Clause:* *Identifying Antecedents*

EXERCISE

F. Underline the adjective clause (or relative clause) in each of the following sentences. Draw a circle around the antecedent it describes.

1. The salmon that inhabit Nova Scotia's lakes and streams are being adversely affected by acid rain.
2. Sharks that swim near beaches can be a danger.
3. Amaranth, which provided food for the Aztecs, may be an important food source for us today.
4. The main noxious component of acid rain is sulfur, which can affect the entire regional ecosystem.
5. The fish that lived here for many years are now extinct.
6. The NMR, which is the first interior observation device with no known adverse side effects, will soon be in use in many hospitals.
7. Any radioactive substance which enters the body can be instrumental in causing cancer.
8. Anything that interferes with the aerodynamics of a car is likely to reduce its fuel efficiency.

COMPREHENSION SKILL INDEX

Relative Clauses (Adjective Clauses) Introduced by *That* or *Which* as Subjects of the Clause

Restrictive and Nonrestrictive

When an adjective clause (relative clause) is set off from the rest of the sentence with commas, it describes the antecedent in general, as a whole class. This type of clause is called "nonrestrictive," because it does not restrict its meaning to one particular thing or to part of a whole class.

example: The shark, which is among the most ancient sea animals, has a very bad
              reputation. (The adjective clause describes sharks in general, or all
              sharks.)

When an adjective clause is not set off from the rest of the sentence with commas, it describes the specific thing named by the antecedent or a part of a larger class. This type of clause is called "restrictive," because it restricts its description to the specific thing named by the antecedent or to part of the class.

examples: The book which contains all the statistics about sulfur emissions
              is no longer in the library.

              The plants which have great commercial value are those with a
              predictable harvest time.

It is obviously important to be aware of whether the adjective clause is restrictive or nonrestrictive, so that you know whether the description it provides refers to all members of the class named by the antecedent, to that specific example only, or to part of the class.

Relative Clauses (Adjective Clauses) Introduced by That *or* Which *as Subjects of the Clause:* Restrictive and Nonrestrictive

EXERCISE

G. The following eleven sentences were taken from the reading on pages 12-14. Draw a circle around the antecedent. Then choose a or b to indicate your understanding of restrictive and nonrestrictive clauses.

1. Although X-rays, which have been in use since 1895, show bones clearly, soft tissues appear fuzzy on the X-ray screen.
   a. describes X-rays in general
   b. only describes those X-rays which have been in use since 1895

2. In recent years a few new diagnostic tools which facilitate interior anatomical observation of soft tissue have emerged.
   a. describes all diagnostic tools
   b. describes just those diagnostic tools that permit interior observation of the body

3. These isotopes are injected into the body in order to detect certain chemical reactions within the body, particularly ones which occur in the brain.
   a. describes just these specific reactions
   b. describes all chemical reactions

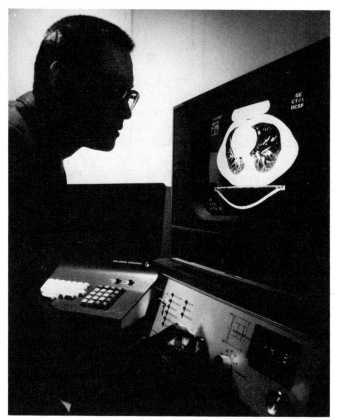

CAT scan image of the vascular patterns within the lung
Courtesy General Electric Research and Development Center

4. They are, however, potentially dangerous, because they make use of the ionizing radiation of X-rays, which in large doses can damage cells and cause infertility.
   a. describes ionizing radiation of X-rays in general
   b. describes just this specific ionizing radiation of X-rays

5. Medical technologists can use the **NMR** to observe processes which are taking place in the tissues and organs.
   a. describes all processes
   b. describes only some specific processes

6. In addition, **NMR** scans are used on patients suffering from multiple sclerosis, which is known as **MS**.
   a. describes multiple sclerosis in general
   b describes just this instance of multiple sclerosis

7. In this disease the fatty myelin sheaths that surround the nerve fibers are worn away and replaced with hard plaques at multiple sites along their length.
   a. describes fatty myelin sheaths in general
   b. describes just these fatty myelin sheaths

8. This is possible because unlike scanners which can only observe cross sections of tissues and organs, the NMR is capable of viewing longitudinal sections of the patient's body.
   a. describes all scanners
   b. describes just some specific kinds of scanners

9. To produce an image, the NMR emits a radio signal that creates a second, or alternating, magnetic force at right angles to the first field.
   a. describes radio signals in general
   b. describes just a specific radio signal

10. Although the NMR may cost more than U.S. $1.5 million each, many medical technologists believe that this is the only scanner that will enable them to do noninvasive internal probing.
    a. describes just this scanner
    b. describes scanners in general

11. [This scanner will enable them to do] noninvasive internal probing to see processes of life which have never before been seen—and to do this safely, without adverse side effects.
    a. describes certain specific life processes
    b. describes life processes in general

Vocabulary Review

EXERCISE

H. The following exercise checks your knowledge of some very important vocabulary which was presented in Book 1 of this series. If you did not use Book 1, see if you need to learn these words. You may find you already know them. Mark the following statements T if they correctly use the italicized review vocabulary words taken from the reading, or F, if they do not.

_____ 1. When something *emerges,* it joins something else and attaches itself to it.

_____ 2. A *scanner* is used to watch something carefully.

_____ 3. "Find" is a word with a meaning similar to *detect.*

_____ 4. If we say that a condition is *potentially* dangerous, we know without a doubt that it is always dangerous.

_____ 5. If you *suffer* from a disease, you have that disease.

_____ 6. *Fatty* substances can be dissolved in water.

_____ 7. When you *monitor* a seismograph, you look at it closely many times.

_____ 8. An *image* is a machine.

A patient undergoing a conventional chest X-ray
American Cancer Society

_____ 9. To *emit* something is to take it in.

_____ 10. An electromagnetic *signal* is a train.

_____ 11. A *field* is an area of force; for example, an electrical field, a magnetic field, or a gravitational field.

_____ 12. When a shark's teeth drop out, they are *replaced* with new ones.

_____ 13. A *buildup* of plaque is an accumulation of plaque.

_____ 14. *Coronary* is a word often associated with agriculture.

_____ 15. *Observing* is an activity related to serving.

_____ 16. To *indicate* is almost the same as to show.

Improving Industrial Efficiency Through Robotics

Automobile spot welding performed by robots

Subtechnical Vocabulary

adjunct (noun)

> helper or assistant who works under the direction of others

> This student is trying to get a summer job as an **adjunct** in the physics lab.

intervention (noun)

> participation; involvement for the purpose of affecting the outcome of something

> Although babies can be born without medical **intervention**, it is a good idea for a doctor to be present in case complications occur.

assembly line (noun)

> place to perform a consecutive series of mechanical manipulations necessary in the manufacturing process; the workers on that line

> The **assembly line** has been used for decades in the automobile manufacturing industry.

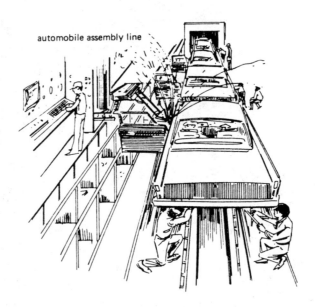

automobile assembly line

pray (noun)

> liquid in droplet form; aerosol; liquid propelled from an atomizer or pressurized container

Above ocean waves there is often a fine **spray**.

spray

appliance (noun)

an electrical tool or device, often for home use

Toasters, refrigerators, washing machines, and air conditioners are **appliances**.

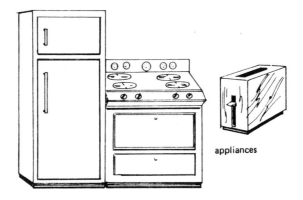

appliances

stack (noun)

neat vertical pile of similar objects

This storage area contains **stacks** of boxes.

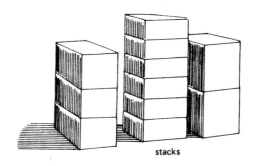

stacks

exposure (noun)

> presence without protection in a dangerous situation

> It is important to limit our **exposure** to X-rays and radioactive substances.

to discard (verb)

> to throw away; to reject

> The space shuttle **is not discarded** after use; it is reusable.

to assemble (verb)

> to put the various parts of a thing together; to manufacture by combining and attaching all the necessary parts

> The more parts an object has, the longer it takes **to assemble** it.

assembling a toy plane

to program (verb)

> to give problem-solving instructions to a computer

> Today computers **are programmed** to do all sorts of calculations and other operations.

to cast (verb)

> to form a substance into a particular shape by pouring it into a mold and letting it harden

> Steel **is cast** to make the frame of a car.

to handle (verb)

> to manipulate; to operate or touch with the hands

> On an assembly line most workers specialize in one task and therefore **handle** very few tools.

digital (adjective)

> related to digits, or numerals

> **Digital** computers perform operations on numerical data in solving problems.

sensitive (adjective)

> responsive to a stimulus that is perceived by the senses; capable of perceiving sounds, tastes, smells, sights, and/or sensations

> Photographic film is **sensitive** to light.

defective (adjective)

> imperfect; having serious manufacturing errors

> **Defective** cars are often recalled by the manufacturer for repairs.

articulated (adjective/past participle)

> having joints or connected segments

> Human arms and human legs are **articulated**.

prevalent (adjective)

> common; often seen

> Carcinoma of the lung is still not as **prevalent** in women as it is in men, but this may not always be true.

versatile (adjective)

> flexible; adaptable; capable of performing a variety of roles well

> Aspirin is a **versatile** drug: It is used with effectiveness as an anti-inflammatory and an anticoagulative.

Vocabulary of Ideas

to take over (phrasal verb)

> to assume control of or take responsibility for

> The adjuncts **have taken over** the management of the laboratory.

to spare (verb)

> to prevent harm from happening to someone; to save someone from pain or injury

> By cutting down on industrial sulfur emissions, we **can spare** the fish population the hazard of acid rain.

in between (expression)

    that which appears between two points on a scale or in a range

    Red and blue are two primary colors; the colors **in between** are shades of violet.

Vocabulary Exercises

A. Match each word in column a with its definition in column b.

a	*b*
1. stack	numerical
2. discard	form by pouring
3. articulated	pile
4. cast	assistant
5. digital	jointed
6. adjunct	reject

B. Complete each statement with a word defined at the beginning of the lesson.

1. Colds are spread through the _____ of droplets released by sneezing and coughing.

2. A seismometer is _____ to movements of the earth's crust that occur even very far away.

3. The NMR _____ the patient from exposure to X-rays and radio-active substances.

4. Because of the risk of infection, it is not good to _____ a skin burn.

5. Most cars are _____ by a combination of humans and machines.

6. _____ to some noxious substances can result in cancer.

7. Landsat is _____ to take continuous pictures of the surface of the earth.

8. The NMR scanner is more _____ than an X-ray machine; it is not limited to cross-sectional views of the body.

C. Choose the correct lettered response to complete each numbered statement.

1. When something does not work as it should, it may either be _____ or improperly used.
    a. prevalent
    b. versatile

c. defective

d. adjunct

2. A(n) _____ such as a vacuum cleaner can save us time at home.

a. appliance

b. spray

c. assembly line

d. intervention

3. I like big cars and small cars, but I don't like those _____.

a. defective

b. versatile

c. to take over

d. in between

4. In many developed nations more and more of the responsibility for assisting at

childbirth is being _____ by nurse-midwives.

a. taken over

b. articulated

c. programmed

d. sensitive

5. At this point, almost everyone agrees that some _____ is needed to stop the acid rain problem from worsening.

a. spray

b. intervention

c. adjunct

d. stack

6. The NMR is not yet the most _____ scanner, but it may well be the best.

a. programmed

b. digital

c. versatile

d. prevalent

7. Most modern factories use the _____ method for manufacturing multi-component machines.

a. adjunct

b. intervention

c. assembly line

d. defective

COMPREHENSION SKILL INDEX

Scanning

You will remember that scanning is the skill you use when you want to find specific information quickly. In scanning, it is a good idea to let your eyes travel very quickly over the entire selection. If you are looking for numbers or numerical statistics, it is not necessary to run your eyes over every line. Numbers visibly jump out among words, so all you need to do is focus briefly on each paragraph to see if the information you want is there.

If you are looking for nonnumerical information, it is a good idea to have a key word in your mind that will serve as a signal that you have found the place where the information is presented. For example, if you are looking for the application of NMR technology to MS patients in the selection on pages 12-14, you will find it quickly by searching for the term *multiple sclerosis, MS,* or even *sclerosis* alone.

Scanning

EXERCISE

D. In the reading on pages 33-34, find the sentences that tell you the answers to the following questions. Then write each sentence in the space provided.

1. What will the value of the robotics industry be by the early 1990s? _____

_____

_____

_____

2. What do robots do in nuclear power plants? _____

_____

_____

_____

3. What kinds of cameras are now used by robots? _____

_____

_____

_____

4. What is the numerical range of brightness values in the gray-scale system used by the robot vision system? _____

_____

_____

5. What are two assembly line operations in the automotive industry? _____

_____

_____

Suffixes

The following class 2 suffixes form adjectives, usually from nouns, but occasionally from other adjectives. One pair *(-able, -ible)* forms adjectives from verbs.

-al, -ical

Noun	Adjective
agriculture	agricultural
commerce	commercial
convention	conventional
face	facial
industry	industrial
instrument	instrumental
margin	marginal
mathematics	mathematical
optics	optical
race	racial
region	regional
tradition	traditional

-able, -ible

Verb	Adjective
flex	flexible
respond	responsible
transport	transportable

-ar

Noun	Adjective
angle	angular
circle	circular
molecule	molecular
nucleus	nuclear

-ic, (-ical)

Noun	Adjective
acid	acidic
alcohol	alcoholic
atom	atomic
atmosphere	atmospheric
base	basic
economy	economic
magnet	magnetic
organ	organic
robot	robotic
science	scientific

-ish

Noun or Adjective	Adjective
black	blackish
fever	feverish
man	mannish
woman	womanish
yellow	yellowish

Intricate painting tasks are carried out by humans before the car enters the automated painting area.

Courtesy General Motors

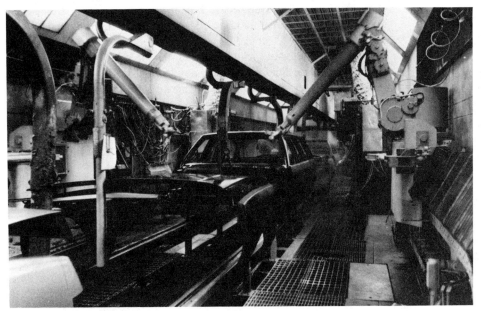

Automatic spray painting of a car on an assembly line

Courtesy General Motors

Reading Selection

Improving Industrial Efficiency Through Robotics

Robots, becoming an increasingly **prevalent adjunct** in factories and industrial plants throughout the developed world, are programmed and engineered mechanical manipulators designed to perform industrial tasks without human **intervention**.   1

Most of today's robots are employed in the automotive industry, where they **are programmed to take over** such **assembly line** operations as welding and **spray** painting automobile and truck bodies. They also load and unload hot, heavy metal forms used in machines **casting** auto and truck frames. In addition, they install bulbs in instrument panels.   2

Robots, already taking over human tasks in the automotive field, are beginning to be seen, although to a lesser degree, in other industries as well. There they build electric motors, small **appliances**, typewriters, pocket calculators, and even watches. The robots used   3 in nuclear power plants **handle** the radioactive materials, **sparing** human personnel **exposure** to radiation. These are the robots responsible for the reduction in job-related injuries in this new industry.

What makes a robot a robot and not just another kind of automatic machine? Robots differ from automatic machines in that after completion of one specific task, they can be reprogrammed by a computer to do another one. As an example, a robot doing spot welding one month can be reprogrammed and switched to spray painting the next. Automatic machines, on the other hand, are less **versatile**; they are built to perform only one task. Robots are more flexible and adaptable and usually more transportable than other machines.

4

Future Robots Will See, Touch, and Think

The next generation of robots will be able to see objects, will have a sense of touch, and will make critical decisions. Engineers skilled in microelectronics and computer technology are developing artificial vision for robots. With the ability to "see," robots can identify and inspect one specific class of objects out of a **stack** of different kinds of materials. One robot vision system uses electronic **digital** cameras containing many rows of light-**sensitive** materials. When light from an object such as a machine part strikes the camera, the sensitive materials measure the intensity of light and convert the light rays into a range of numbers. The numbers are part of a gray-scale system in which brightness is measured in a range of values. One scale ranges from 0 to 15, and another from 0 to 255. The 0 is represented by black. The highest number is white. The numbers **in between** represent different shades of gray. The computer then makes the calculations and converts the numbers into a picture that shows an image of the object in question. It is not yet known whether robots will one day have vision as good as human vision. Technicians believe they will, but only after years of development.

5

Engineers working on other advances are designing and experimenting with new types of **articulated** metal hands and fingers, giving robots a sense of touch. Other engineers are writing new programs allowing robots to make decisions such as whether to **discard defective** parts in finished products. To do this, the robot will also have to be capable of identifying those defective parts.

6

These future robots, **assembled** with a sense of touch and the ability to see and make decisions, will have plenty of work to do. They can be used to prospect for minerals on the ocean floor or in deep areas of mines too dangerous for humans to enter. They will work as gas station attendants, firefighters, housekeepers, and security personnel. The robot business will continue to grow also. Financial analysts believe this business will soar from a U.S. $100-million industry at the start of the 1980s to a U.S. $5-billion industry by the early 1990s. Anyone wanting to understand the industry of the future will have to know about robotics.

7

Comprehension

E. Mark the following statements T if they are true or F if they are false.

_____ 1. More and more robots are being employed in industry.

_____ 2. Robots need humans to supervise all their movements.

_____ 3. The majority of robots are currently in the painting business.

_____ 4. Robots take bulbs out of cars' instrument panels.

_____ 5. Robots at present are limited to the automobile industry.

_____ 6. Robots operate small appliances and type on typewriters.

_____ 7. Robots in nuclear power plants do everything but handle radioactive materials.

_____ 8. Robots are programmed by computers.

_____ 9. Robots are more versatile than conventional automatic machines.

_____ 10. Robots are less transportable than other machines.

_____ 11. Soon robots will be able to assess the quality of a group of stacked items.

_____ 12. The gray-scale system is used by robots to convert relative brightness to images.

_____ 13. Robotics has many potential applications.

Vocabulary in Context

EXERCISE

F. Choose the correct lettered response to define each numbered word.

1. completion (¶ 4)
   a. finishing
   b. beginning
2. switched (¶ 4)
   a. changed
   b. electrified
3. vision (¶ 5)
   a. light
   b. sight

4. values (¶ 5)
   a. beliefs
   b. numbers
5. prospect (¶ 7)
   a. future
   b. dig
6. soar (¶ 7)
   a. decrease
   b. grow

Drawing Conclusions

EXERCISE

G. Choose a or b to answer each question.

1. Why is decreased human intervention desirable?
   a. because it cuts down on costs
   b. because humans make too many defective items
2. Why are robots a good choice for loading and unloading the auto- and truck-casting forms?
   a. because they cannot get burned
   b. because the work is boring
3. Why were robots introduced first into automobile manufacturing plants?
   a. because they are well suited to assembly line tasks
   b. because someday they will drive cars
4. Why can robots handle radioactive materials without danger?
   a. because they are well protected by their metal suits
   b. because they are not living things
5. What causes most injuries in nuclear power plants?
   a. exposure to radiation
   b. the newness of the industry
6. Why is it so important for robots to be able to "see"?
   a. so they can criticize human factory personnel
   b. so they can make critical decisions
7. What kinds of tasks are robots most suitable for?
   a. boring, repetitive, and dangerous tasks
   b. difficult tasks
8. Why will those people interested in industry have to know about robotics?
   a. because robots will become very prevalent in industry
   b. so they can make a lot of money

Reduced Adjective (Relative) Clauses

Adjective clauses are very commonly reduced to shorter adjective phrases in scientific and technical writing. This happens more frequently when *that* and *which* serve as objects in the clause, although it may also occur when they serve as subjects.

examples: The scanners that are used in most hospitals are not magnetic scanners.

The scanners used in most hospitals are not magnetic scanners.

The sharks that are swimming in the area today will probably not be here tomorrow.

The sharks swimming in the area today will probably not be here tomorrow.

The household appliance that is responsible for the biggest time saving is the automatic washing machine.

The household appliance responsible for the biggest time saving is the automatic washing machine.

The personnel that are on the assembly line will go home at five o'clock.

The personnel on the assembly line will go home at five o'clock.

This hospital's scanners, which include three CAT scanners and one PET scanner, are all in use.

This hospital's scanners, including three CAT scanners and one PET scanner, are all in use.

Note that the comma setting off nonrestrictive information is used in the same way in the reduced form.

Often in scientific and technical writing, the key to understanding the prevalent long sentences is recognizing and understanding the full meaning of the reduced adjective clause (adjective phrase).

The reading on pages 33-34 contains a total of seventeen reduced adjective clauses within thirteen sentences. Note that clauses 1 and 2, 3 and 4, 10 and 11, and 14 and 15 occur as pairs in the same sentence. This is also something you will need to become familiar with; such pairing occurs frequently in scientific and technical writing.

Reduced Adjective (Relative) Clauses

EXERCISES

H. Find the thirteen sentences that contain the seventeen adjective clauses in the reading on pages 33-34. Write them below and circle the antecedent to each phrase. Then underline each adjective phrase.

1. _____

   _____

   _____

2. _____

   _____

   _____

3. _____

   _____

   _____

Telephone assembly on a conventional assembly line

A.T. & T. Co. Photo Center

4. _____
   _____
   _____

5. _____
   _____
   _____

6. _____
   _____
   _____

7. _____
   _____
   _____

8. _____
   _____
   _____

9. _____
   _____
   _____

10. _____
    _____
    _____

11. _____
    _____
    _____

12. _____
    _____
    _____

13. _____
    _____
    _____

I. Using *which* or *that* and making any necessary changes, convert the reduced adjective phrases back to adjective clauses. Follow the model.

model: Robots, already taking over human tasks in the automotive field, are beginning to be seen, although to a lesser degree, in other industries as well. ⟶
Robots, which are already taking over human tasks in the automotive field, are beginning to be seen, although to a lesser degree, in other industries as well.

1. _____

_____

2. _____

_____

3. _____

_____

4. _____

_____

5. _____

_____

6. _____

_____

7. _____

_____

8. _____

_____

9. _____

_____

10. _____

_____

11. _____

_____

12. _____

_____

13. _____

_____

Reading Numbers in English

Unlike most languages, English uses a comma to separate the hundreds groups in large numbers.

example: 3,675,890

English uses the period to indicate a decimal.

example: 5.67% (read: five point six seven percent)

Note that the word *billion* in American English indicates one thousand million, that is, 1,000,000,000.

In American English each set of three zeros makes a number of a new name. A trillion is 1,000,000,000,000; a quadrillion is 1,000,000,000,000,000, and so on. If you are using materials published in the U.K., the naming of some numbers will be different.

example:

	U.S.	*U.K.*
million	6 zeros	6 zeros
milliard	(not used)	9 zeros
billion	9 zeros	12 zeros
trillion	12 zeros	18 zeros
quadrillion	15 zeros	24 zeros

Reading Numbers in English

EXERCISE

J. Write the number for each of the following, according to American usage.

1. thirteen thousand twenty-one _____

2. ten point two per cent _____

3. one million, five hundred fifty-five thousand, two hundred thirty-six _____

_____

4. one sextillion _____

5. two million _____

Adaptation to the Environment Promotes Survival: The Barn Owl

A barn owl entering a tree nest with a captured mouse

Subtechnical Vocabulary

investigation (noun)

research; study that is directed toward finding out how or why something occurs

It is hoped that the **investigation** of shark's blood will result in the identification of a cancer-inhibiting factor.

shelter (noun)

place that prevents exposure to harmful conditions; a structure that provides protection from the weather

The three most basic needs we have are food, water, and **shelter**.

An umbrella provides shelter from the rain.

remains (noun)

what is left after use or destruction of all the other parts

They left in a hurry, not stopping to discard the **remains** of their meal.

camouflage (noun)

protective coloration of an animal or a plant

One of the factors enabling most animals of prey to be successful is **camouflage**.

surroundings (noun)

environment, particularly in the physical sense

The **surroundings** of every living thing affect its development.

homogeneous (adjective)

all of one type; uniform in composition

The population of fish in this lake is virtually **homogeneous**; over 99 percent of the fish are salmon.

trough (noun)

a depression in the surface, providing a passageway or a collecting place

A **trough** is found between successive waves in the ocean.

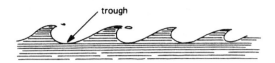

stationary (adjective)

unmoving; incapable of moving; fixed to prevent movement

Buildings are **stationary**, while cars move.

intense (adjective)

concentrated; vigorous in effort

Toxic waste emissions require immediate and **intense** study.

subtle (adjective)

slight; difficult to perceive

Seasonal temperature changes are more **subtle** near the equator than they are in the extreme south of the southern hemisphere.

intricate (adjective)

complicated; difficult to perceive the separate elements of; having many complexities

The circulatory system is an **intricate** network of many different kinds of blood vessels.

to ascertain (verb)

to find out by investigation

Once the diagnosis of a disease **is ascertained**, treatment can begin.

to regurgitate (verb)

to cough up or vomit undigested substances from the stomach

Cows and other bovines **regurgitate** food as a part of their digestive process.

to blend in with (phrasal verb)

to appear homogeneous with one's surroundings

Camouflage enables an animal **to blend in with** its environment.

to confirm (verb)

to provide data supporting an idea; to verify; to establish with information

Researchers expect **to confirm** soon that arterial plaque removal can be carried out without surgery.

to funnel (verb)

to channel a substance from a large collecting place through a small space and into another container

In filling a test tube from a large bottle, it is a good idea **to funnel** the material, so that it will be more controllable and less likely to spill.

to funnel

to evolve (verb)

to develop by natural selection, for example, a species

Plants and animals **evolved** from simple one-celled organisms over millions and millions of years.

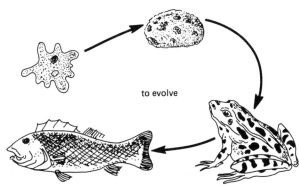

to evolve

to infer (verb)

> to guess or determine from study, logic, or sensory information
>
> We can often **infer** an object's composition by touching it.

to promote (verb)

> to aid in; to support; to advance
>
> Heavy sugar consumption **promotes** tooth decay.

Vocabulary of Ideas

chiefly (adverb)

> mostly; mainly; essentially
>
> The industrial pollutants causing acid rain are **chiefly** those containing sulfur.

so far (adverbial expression)

> until now; until then
>
> The only thing we know **so far** is that sharks don't get cancer; but we don't yet know precisely why.

to belong (verb)

> to be a part of; to be a possession of
>
> Industrial sulfur emissions **belong** to the category of pollutants that can do damage far away from their source.

to comprise (verb)

> to include; to contain; to be composed of
>
> The class Mammalia **comprises** all animals that feed their young the milk produced in their bodies.

to share (verb)

> to participate in or use together or in common
>
> Although sharks and bony fish **share** certain characteristics, for example, general shape and the ability to swim, the differences between them are numerous.

propensity (noun)

> inclination; habit; liking
>
> It has been shown that sharks have a **propensity** for certain colors.

Vocabulary Exercises

A. Complete the following sentences with words from the list.

promotes	remains	comprises	camouflage	subtle
stationary	belongs	investigation	so far	share

1. Amaranth _____ to that group of wild plants having promise as potential food crops.

2. It is widely believed that a high fat diet _____ arterial plaque buildup.

3. It is almost impossible to see a camouflaged animal that remains _____ in its usual surroundings.

4. The term *scanner* now _____ the CAT, the PET, and the new NMR.

5. There is a _____ difference in meaning between the words *surroundings* and *environment.*

6. _____ of automobile aerodynamics has led to many design improvements.

7. The _____ of something are generally of no further use.

8. All living things _____ certain traits: metabolism, growth, irritability, and reproduction.

9. _____ provides an interesting illustration of the evolutionary process.

10. Progress in the cancer field has been limited _____ to the treatment, rather than the prevention, of the disease.

B. Choose the correct lettered response to complete each numbered statement.

1. In severe weather adequate _____ is extremely important.
   a. shelter
   b. camouflage

2. Chemical bonding often occurs when two molecules have a _____ for each other.
   a. propensity
   b. trough

3. Until now, noninvasive procedures for viewing the interior of the body consisted _____ of X-rays.
   a. so far
   b. chiefly

4. The population of Sweden is more _____ than the population of the United States.
   a. intricate
   b. homogeneous

5. It has been _____ that X-rays, in large doses, are carcinogenic.
   a. promoted
   b. ascertained

6. Severe earthquakes can cause _____ tremors in the earth's crust for a great distance.
   a. intense
   b. stationary

7. When animals are very frightened, they sometimes _____ the remains of their food to prepare them for fight or flight.
   a. regurgitate
   b. share

8. The liftoff of a rocket occurs after an _____ series of completed steps.
   a. intricate
   b. homogeneous

9. Many tropical fish have coloration that evolved to help them _____ the bright colors of their environment.
   a. belong to
   b. blend in with

10. If all the children in a school were to become sick one hour after lunch, it would be reasonable to _____ that the food they ate was responsible for their illness.
    a. infer
    b. ascertain

11. It is a mistake to infer that humans have stopped _____ merely because we have not observed changes during our history.
    a. evolving
    b. comprising

12. In the casting process, first the hot liquid steel is _____ from the large foundry to the smaller molds.
    a. regurgitated
    b. funneled

13. A canal and a river bed are like a _____; they provide a passageway via a surface depression.
    a. trough
    b. shelter

14. Changes in the _____ always affect the organisms that live there.
    a. surroundings
    b. camouflage

15. These new data _____ what we had previously inferred.
    a. evolve
    b. confirm

Understanding Vocabulary from Word Parts

Suffixes

The following class 2 suffixes convert nouns to other nouns or to adjectives.

-ful

Noun	Adjective
box	boxful
cup	cupful
hand	handful
mouth	mouthful

-less

Noun	Adjective
bottom	bottomless
insect	insectless
motion	motionless
point	pointless
rain	rainless
shelter	shelterless
top	topless
tremor	tremorless
water	waterless
wind	windless

The following pairs of adjectives are antonyms created by the addition of *-ful* or *-less* to the same noun.

Noun	Adjective	Adjective
care	careful	careless
event	eventful	eventless
fear	fearful	fearless
pain	painful	painless
power	powerful	powerless

Adaptation to the Environment Promotes Survival: The Barn Owl   **49**

thought	thoughtful	thoughtless
use	useful	useless

-ly

Noun	Adjective (some also serve as adverbs)
day	daily
death	deathly
earth	earthly
friend	friendly
hour	hourly
man	manly
month	monthly
scholar	scholarly
week	weekly
woman	womanly
year	yearly

-y

Noun	Adjective
dew	dewy
feather	feathery
gas	gassy
glass	glassy
grass	grassy
ice	icy
mud	muddy
salt	salty
snow	snowy
soup	soupy
sugar	sugary
worm	wormy

Young barn owls in the nest
Interior-Sport Fisheries and Wildlife

Reading Selection

Adaptation to the Environment Promotes Survival: The Barn Owl

Barn owls represent an interesting example of what adaptation to the environment means. These birds, found in tropical and temperate climates throughout the world, are currently the subject of **intense investigation** by ornithologists, who are finding out if the owls use hearing, as opposed to sight, in capturing their prey. **1**

The barn owl family **belongs** to the order Strigiformes, a **homogeneous** order **comprising** all owls. What distinguishes owls from other birds of prey (such as hawks, for example) is their **propensity** for nocturnal activity and the **stationary** forward-directedness of their eyes. What owls **share** with other birds of prey are a hooked beak, strong legs, and sharp talons. **2**

We know that the favorite habitat of the barn owl is the barn. That is, in fact, where it gets its name. Other frequent roosting places for barn owls are in the hollows of trees, in rock piles, and under the **shelter** of tall reeds. The birds hunt **chiefly** in large open **3**

hooked: bent and turned downward

beak: bony external mouth part of birds

talons: claws; sharp-nailed feet

reeds: grasses

areas such as fields, and decide where to breed only once—they breed yearly in the same place.

Investigators have observed that the barn owl **regurgitates** the indigestible **remains** of its food. From this material they have **ascertained** which items make up the bird's primary food. They know that it feeds mainly on small vertebrates, especially rodents, but also on worms and insects. Its favorite prey are smaller mammals—mainly field mice. Catching field mice is not an easy task, because these little animals forage for food mostly at night when it is dark. Furthermore, field mice are **camouflaged, blending in** well **with** their **surroundings.** What makes things even more difficult is that the mice know how to burrow through grass, hay, or snow to keep out of sight. For these reasons they are difficult or impossible to see, even though barn owls have keen eyesight. The barn owls, therefore, must know exactly when and where to strike.

4

Ornithologists wanted to **confirm** whether the barn owl catches its prey by sound alone. They investigated the anatomical structure of the bird's skull and head to understand how this might be possible. They found that the bird's heart-shaped facial ruff is composed of rows of tightly packed feathers. The facial ruff acts like a surface disk that helps collect and concentrate high-frequency sound waves. It has been shown that the bird's external ears are actually **troughs** that run through the ruff from the lower beak to the forehead: a distance of 9 centimeters. These external ears are what collects sounds from a large volume of space and **funnels** them into the ear canals.

5

The results of these studies indicate that the barn owl is able to perceive sounds, both horizontally and vertically, better than any other animal **so far** tested. They have superbly **evolved** ears. The right ear and trough are tilted upward, making them more adaptable to picking up sounds coming from above. The left ear and trough are tilted downward, and are more adaptable to collecting sounds coming from below. The ear nearer the location where the sound is coming from will receive the sound of higher intensity. Assessing these **subtle** differences in sound intensity is how the bird **infers** the location of its prey—the bird can even detect sudden changes in the prey's direction.

6

The ability of the barn owl to hunt by sound alone is an example of how adaptation promotes survival. Its adaptation to the realities of its surroundings illustrates that **intricate** differences distinguish one living organism from another, and makes us understand how these differences have enabled each kind of organism to survive.

7

rodents: small furry animals, e.g., rats

worms: small, long, legless crawling animals

disk: round, flat object

Comprehension

EXERCISE

C. Mark the following statements T if they are true or F if they are false.

_____ 1. Barn owls live in all climate zones of the world.

_____ 2. Ornithologists want to determine what means the owl uses in hunting.

_____ 3. Many different kinds of birds make up the order Strigiformes.

_____ 4. Hawks, like owls, habitually are most active at night.

_____ 5. Hawks do not have stationary eyes.

_____ 6. Owls, unlike other birds of prey, have sharp talons.

_____ 7. The barn owl hunts mainly inside barns.

_____ 8. Each year the barn owl finds a new breeding place.

_____ 9. The diet of the barn owl is known.

_____ 10. The barn owl eats rodents, worms, and insects.

_____ 11. Field mice are easy to capture.

_____ 12. Field mice are nocturnal.

_____ 13. Barn owls cannot see well.

_____ 14. The owl's face is square.

_____ 15. The facial ruff increases the bird's ability to hear.

_____ 16. The external ears are a depression in the feathers.

_____ 17. The owl's face is approximately 9 centimeters long.

_____ 18. The ear canals funnel the sound into the ruff.

_____ 19. The barn owl has superb hearing.

_____ 20. The two ears are identical.

_____ 21. The owl locates its prey by measuring slight differences in sound intensity.

Vocabulary in Context

EXERCISE

D. Find the *one* word in the indicated paragraph that is closest to being a synonym to the word or expression given below.

1. owls (¶ 1): _____

2. bird specialists (¶ 1): _____

3. catching (¶ 1): _____

4. other birds of prey (¶ 2): _____

5. nighttime (¶ 2): _____

6. living place (¶ 3): _____

7. sitting or perching (¶ 3): _____

8. look for and catch prey (¶ 3): _____

9. small vertebrates (¶ 4): _____

10. search (¶ 4): _____

11. tunnel (¶ 4): _____

12. hit (¶ 4): _____

13. surface made of feathers (¶ 5): _____

14. turned (¶ 6): _____

COMPREHENSION SKILL INDEX | Noun Clauses

Review the functions of nouns within sentences. Nouns function as subjects, objects, and predicates.

examples: subject

Science is interesting.

object (of verb)

I like science

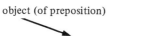

object (of preposition)

The area of science that I like best is chemistry.

predicate

My favorite subject is science.

Noun clauses are used heavily in scientific and technical writing. They perform the same grammatical functions as nouns, serving as subjects, objects, and predicates.

examples:

subject

How you perform your research is important.

object

No one knows what causes cancer.

predicate

That is exactly what we want to know.

Noun clauses are usually introduced by *that, if, whether,* and the following interrogative words: *how, what, when, where, which, who, whom, whose,* and *why.*

examples: We have just learned *that the hospital purchased an NMR scanner.*

Amaranth is *what agronomists are planning to cultivate* in the near future.

That lasers have so many medical uses is very exciting.

The speaker didn't say *whether sulfur emissions would be controlled or not.*

We don't know *if amaranth cultivation will ever be economically feasible.*

We can only guess *how robots will be used in industry.*

I tried to ascertain *what the cause of the buildup was.*

There is currently no reliable way to predict *when an earthquake will occur.*

Where one will occur is easier to predict.

We don't know *which element will be most efficient in the newer solar cells.*

Did you ask your professor *who discovered X-rays*?

He didn't say *whom he had spoken to.*

I can't say *whose test results are better.*

They don't know *why sharks sometimes attack swimmers.*

Noun Clauses

E. There are twenty-four noun clauses in the following sentences taken from the reading on pages 51-52. Underline each noun clause. Then, above each clause, label it a subject, object, or predicate, as the case may be.

1. Barn owls represent an interesting example of what adaptation to the environment means.

2. These birds, found in tropical and temperate climates throughout the world, are currently the subject of intense investigation by ornithologists, who are finding out if the owls use hearing, as opposed to sight, in capturing their prey.

3. What distinguishes owls from other birds of prey (such as hawks, for example) is their propensity for nocturnal activity and the stationary forward-directedness of their eyes.

4. What owls share with other birds of prey are a hooked beak, strong legs, and sharp talons.

5. We know that the favorite habitat of the barn owl is the barn.

6. That is, in fact, where it gets its name.

7. The birds hunt chiefly in large open areas, such as fields, and decide where to breed only once.

8. Investigators have observed that the barn owl regurgitates the indigestible remains of its food.

9. From this material they have ascertained which items make up the bird's primary food.

10. They know that it feeds mainly on small vertebrates, especially rodents, but also on worms and insects.

11.-13. What makes things even more difficult is that the mice know how to burrow through grass, hay, or snow to keep themselves out of sight.

14. The barn owls, therefore, must know exactly when and where to strike.

15. Ornithologists wanted to confirm whether the barn owl catches its prey by sound alone.

16. They investigated the anatomical structure of the bird's skull and head to understand how this might be possible.

17. They found that the bird's heart-shaped facial ruff is composed of rows of tightly packed feathers.

18. It has been shown that the bird's external ears are actually troughs that run through the ruff from the lower beak to the forehead.

19. These external ears are what collects sounds from a large volume of space and funnels them into the ear canals.

20. The results of these studies indicate that the barn owl is able to perceive sounds, both horizontally and vertically, better than any other animal so far tested.

21. Assessing these subtle differences in sound intensity is how the bird infers the location of its prey.

22. The ability of the barn owl to hunt by sound alone is an example of how adaptation promotes survival.

23.-24. The adaptation of the barn owl to the realities of its surroundings illustrates that intricate differences distinguish one living organism from another, and makes us understand how these differences have enabled each kind of organism to survive.

The barn owl
Interior-U.S. Fish and Wildlife Service

One-Person Submersibles in Oceanographic Mineral Exploration

A deep-water submersible being released

Subtechnical Vocabulary

accessibility (noun)

availability; reachability

Laser technology makes **accessibility** to the interior of arteries a noninvasive procedure.

sediment (noun)

solid material found on the bottom of a quantity of liquid; the earth deposited under a body of water

Over the years **sediment** is deposited on the ocean floor.

sediment on the ocean floor

mean (noun)

the average number; the number obtained by taking the sum of all the numbers in the set and dividing it by the number of individual items in the set

The **mean** of 7, 10, and 18 is $11\frac{2}{3}$.

syndrome (noun)

recognized set of undesirable physical symptoms and signs which appear together

Hypoglycemia, or low blood sugar, is a **syndrome** consisting of weakness, irritability, and overweight.

exploitation (noun)

consumption or use, particularly of a resource or a technology, for the greatest possible advantage or most complete use

The heavy **exploitation** of laser technology has reduced the number of eye operations in recent years.

ore (noun)

a mineral from which a metal can be mined or extracted

Steel is made from iron **ore**.

coma (noun)

state of deep unconsciousness caused by injury, poison, or disease

Coma is a very grave condition with poor survival potential.

gear (noun)

special clothing or equipment necessary for a specific task

Diving **gear** includes rubberized suits, air tanks, and masks.

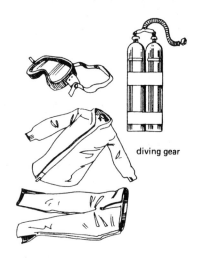

diving gear

apparatus (noun)

device; machine or group of machines designed to accomplish a specific task

The "Canada," the manipulating arm aboard the space shuttle, is an **apparatus** used for moving objects in the cargo bay.

sample (noun)

piece or portion of a substance to be studied, chosen because it represents the whole

Often a doctor takes a blood **sample** for study.

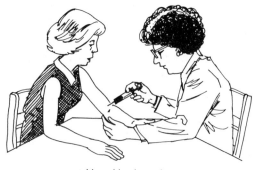

taking a blood sample

to exceed (verb)

to be greater than

When the acid level of lake water **exceeds** a certain point, fish begin to die.

to last (verb)

to continue to exist; to endure

A cold **lasts** for about a week.

to ascend (verb)

to go up; to climb

After working on the ocean floor, the deep-sea diver **ascends** slowly to the surface.

to ascend

to exert (verb)

to impose; to put into force

The atmosphere **exerts** a higher pressure at sea level than it does on the top of high mountains.

to withstand (verb)

to survive by resisting something or by using force against something

The rubberized suits divers wear enable them **to withstand** the low temperatures in their surroundings.

gradual (adjective)

slow; step-by-step

A **gradual** process does not occur from one day to another; it takes place in small steps over a period of time.

constant (adjective)

unchanging

Pressurization in passenger aircraft provides a **constant** atmospheric pressure for the comfort and safety of the passengers and crew.

innovative (adjective)

presenting, introducing, or creatively making use of the newest technology

The most **innovative** car designs result from aerodynamic research.

in direct proportion to

with relation to; happening in relation to the occurrence of something else

Plants grow **in direct proportion to** the amount of sunlight they get.

Vocabulary of Ideas

to constitute (verb)

to make up; to compose; to represent

The CAT, the PET, and the NMR **constitute** the most often used scanning devices.

to appreciate (verb)

to realize; to understand; to be fully aware of

Although we **appreciate** the hazards frequent X-rays pose, the potential benefits are so great that we use them when necessary.

largely (adverb)

mainly; chiefly; on a large scale

Sharks are **largely** harmless; only a few species give the animal its fearsome reputation.

some (adverb)

> approximately; about

> **Some** fifty people attended the conference on underwater mineral exploration.

principal (adjective)

> most important

> The **principal** goal of the earth resources technology satellite is the monitoring of our resources.

according to (expression)

> on the statement of or in the opinion of

> **According to** many agronomists, amaranth hybridization may make commercial cultivation of the crop feasible.

Vocabulary Exercises

A. Change the italicized word in each statement to a word defined at the beginning of the lesson.

_____ 1. No special *clothing* is required for university teaching.

_____ 2. It is not difficult to *understand* the importance of industrial sulfur emissions reduction.

_____ 3. The *average* summertime temperature in this city is 20°C.

_____ 4. The *consumption* of our natural resources is a problem everyone is worrying about.

_____ 5. The *main* problem with amaranth is its unpredictable harvest time.

_____ 6. The *deposit* at the bottom of a glass of fruit juice is composed of particles of solid fruit.

_____ 7. The seismograph is a tremor-sensing *device.*

_____ 8. Pain and shortness of breath *make up* the two principal symptoms of heart attacks.

_____ 9. In the temperate regions of the world, seasonal temperature changes are *slow.*

B. Choose the correct lettered response to complete each numbered statement.

1. Skin cancer rates increase _____ proximity to the equator.
   a. in direct proportion to
   b. withstanding
   c. some
   d. largely

2. A set of symptoms constitutes a _____.
   a. means
   b. coma
   c. syndrome
   d. sample

3. _____ many seismologists, earthquake prediction may soon be possible.
   a. Largely
   b. Some
   c. In direct proportion to
   d. According to

4. In a(n) _____ patients are actually near death.
   a. coma
   b. gear
   c. apparatus
   d. syndrome

5. One of the problems in industrial emissions monitoring is that pollutant levels do not
   remain _____ for a long period of time.
   a. gradual
   b. principal
   c. innovative
   d. constant

6. The magnetic force _____ in the guideway causes the forward movement of
   the maglev.
   a. exerted
   b. exceeded
   c. withstood
   d. constituted

7. The most _____ of the earthquake prediction systems involves the measuring
   of radon in ground water.
   a. principal
   b. innovative
   c. gradual
   d. accessible

8. Most fish in lakes polluted with sulfur emissions are unable to _____ the acid water.
   a. withstand
   b. constitute
   c. exert
   d. exceed

9. In order to determine the content of an ore deposit, it is necessary to analyze a(n)

   _____ of the material.
   a. mean
   b. apparatus
   c. sediment
   d. sample

10. In the space shuttle the crew has to _____ from the living quarters into the command module.
    a. constitute
    b. ascend
    c. withstand
    d. appreciate

11. The death of the fish was caused _____ by the raised acidity levels in their surroundings.
    a. largely
    b. in direct proportion
    c. according
    d. gradually

12. _____ 200 lakes in Scandinavia currently have no fish.
    a. Largely
    b. Mean
    c. Constant
    d. Some

13. _____ to the new noninvasive observation apparatuses will make diagnosis much less hazardous.
    a. Accessibility
    b. Syndrome
    c. Sediment
    d. Gear

14. The basking shark often _____ 8 meters in length.
    a. exerts
    b. exceeds
    c. withstands
    d. ascends

15. It is hoped that the benefits of laser arterial plaque vaporization will _____ for many years.
    a. last
    b. withstand
    c. exert
    d. constitute

16. The _____ yield of this mine is lower than we expected.
    a. gear
    b. coma
    c. sediment
    d. ore

COMPREHENSION SKILL INDEX

Understanding Vocabulary from Word Parts

The following class 2 suffixes form adjectives.

-ant, -ent

Verb	Adjective
constitute	constituent
depend	dependent
differ	different
observe	observant

-ive, -ative, (-itive)

Verb	Adjective
appreciate	appreciative
compare	comparative
conserve	conservative
digest	digestive
illustrate	illustrative
instruct	instructive

-ous

Noun	Adjective
disaster	disastrous
hazard	hazardous
nerve	nervous
danger	dangerous
industry	industrious

Diver entering a decompression chamber after deep-sea dive
Institute of Diving

Reading Selection

submersible: craft
capable of operating
at great depths

One-Person Submersibles
in Oceanographic Mineral Exploration

Exploitation of marine resources dates back to antiquity, when salt was first produced from the intentional evaporation of sea water. As of the last part of the twentieth century, the interest in extracting **ore** and raw materials from the sea has grown **in direct proportion to** the growing **accessibility** of the ocean depths provided by emerging high-pressure technology.   1

Oceans cover **some** 70 percent of the earth's surface. Although the **mean** depth of the world's oceans is approximately 4000 meters, ocean depth variability is considerable, with a range including trenches at 10,000- and 11,000-meter depths (in the Kermadec, Izu, Philippine, Kuril, Tonga, and Mariana Trenches of the Pacific).   2

untold: unknown, but
very large

Oceanographers and geologists believe there is an untold wealth of mineral resources in offshore deposits lying in marine **sediments.** Copper, lead, nickel, cobalt, zinc, and manganese **constitute** some of the currently most sought after substances. **According to** one geologist, many of the minerals, such as copper, nickel, and cobalt, **exceed** in quantity known land-based supplies. As an example of the immensity of the stores, there may be enough nickel in the sea bottom **to last** some 150,000 years at the current   3 rate of consumption. Virtually all geologists agree that potential marine mineral yields remain as of the present **largely** unknown.

Marine resource mining and retrieval, however, present numerous challenges. Many mineral deposits lie 3500 to 6000 meters below the ocean's surface. At the 5000- to 6000-meter depth, it is not only cold and dark, but the hydrostatic pressures can reach a crushing more than one-hundred-kilograms-per-square-centimeter force. The need for a safe, comfortable, and cost-effective technology for undersea exploration is obvious.

4

Even under ordinary diving conditions in high-though-survivable pressure areas, divers face a serious **syndrome** called the bends. It occurs when a diver **ascends** too rapidly from a high-pressure area to a low-pressure one. The differential between the sea-bottom pressure and the atmospheric pressure at sea level can be enormous. As an example, the atmosphere **exerts** a one-kilogram-per-square-centimeter pressure at sea level compared with an 11.29-kilograms-per-square-centimeter pressure at a 100-meter depth. This represents a more than tenfold increase and requires great care if dangerous consequences are to be avoided. Divers must go through a lengthy, **gradual** ascent known as decompression to allow their bodies to adapt to the lessening pressure, and therefore avoid the bends. The decompression process promotes a slow release of nitrogen from the blood. If the diver surfaces too rapidly, the bends occurs, and nitrogen bubbles can form in the joints, blood vessels, and brain, causing stomach pains, respiratory difficulties, nervousness, irritability, and even **coma**. If adaptation at these relatively shallow depths is so complicated, it is not difficult **to appreciate** that at the extreme depths in which many minerals are located, human survival would not be possible without protection.

5

High-pressure-submersible construction technology has existed for several decades. Submersible craft capable of operating at a greater than 1.8-kilometer depth limit date from the middle 1960s. In all these craft the crew and instruments are protected from the increased pressures in an approximately 2-meter-diameter metallic sphere. From this sphere, special windows permit visual exploration of the scene outside. Since the interior of the sphere is maintained at **constant** atmospheric conditions, no specialized **gear** and no decompression are necessary. As of the early 1980s, however, the **principal** submersible craft have been mostly government enterprises and are large enough to carry several crew members and extensive instrumentation. The size of these craft, however, has accounted for the relatively low level of maneuverability and for their high cost.

6

New are the prototype one-person submersibles now being constructed. These may eliminate the hazards of deep diving while opening the way for engineers and miners to explore the ocean depths for mineral resources. One such craft being worked on in

tenfold: ten times

enterprises: projects

acrylic: kind of plastic

England has a depth capability of 1500 meters. Design of the craft includes a 1.5-meter-diameter acrylic sphere which is attached to a 2.5-meter body made of aluminum and glass fiber. The craft is engineered **to withstand** a 350-kilogram-per-square-centimeter pressure. At 1500 meters the battery-powered craft has a 3-kilometer-per-hour cruising speed. Probably the most **innovative** device on the submersible will be the 1.2-meter mechanical arm. This **apparatus** will be strong enough to lift heavy **samples,** yet small enough to have the finesse and dexterity of a human arm. Although the larger submersibles already in operation make use of mechanical arms, the one on the new one-person submersibles represents a new generation in this technology, because its smallness provides access to areas previously too small to be explored.

7

cruising speed: normal operating speed when not ascending or descending

finesse: accuracy

The submersible and its mechanical arm will provide all the advantages a free diver has without the corresponding disadvantages of working in cold temperatures in poorly lit areas and having to go through the decompression process before surfacing. Because of these factors, the one-person submersibles may be just the right vehicles for ocean-floor mineral exploration.

8

A scuba diver diving for enjoyment
Institute of Diving

Comprehension

C. Mark the following statements T if they are true or F if they are false.

_____ 1. Salt has only recently been recovered from evaporated sea water.

_____ 2. The ocean depths are more accessible today than they were in the past.

_____ 3. High-pressure technology is a growing field.

_____ 4. Exactly 70 percent of the earth's surface is occupied by oceans.

_____ 5. Ocean depth is a fairly constant 4000 meters.

_____ 6. The deepest trenches can be 11,000 meters deep.

_____ 7. The mineral resources in question lie deep in the earth's crust, below the sea.

_____ 8. There may be more copper in marine sediments than there is on solid ground.

_____ 9. In the last 150,000 years, nickel has been mined on the sea bottom.

_____ 10. We don't actually know the exact quantity of underwater mineral deposits.

_____ 11. Underwater mining is difficult.

_____ 12. Pressure increases in direct proportion to depth.

_____ 13. The bends is a set of symptoms.

_____ 14. The bends occurs when a diver reaches the ocean floor.

_____ 15. Sea-level atmospheric pressure is ten times greater than the hydro-static pressure at a depth of 100 meters.

_____ 16. A gradual ascent is the best means of avoiding the bends.

_____ 17. The nitrogen release rate is slowed by the decompression process.

_____ 18. The bends can be very serious.

_____ 19. One of the symptoms of the bends is blindness.

_____ 20. Submersible craft are extremely new.

_____ 21. There are windows in some submersible craft.

_____ 22. The submersible craft have to ascend slowly so that the crew won't get the bends.

_____ 23. The English prototype is capable of diving very deep.

_____ 24. No other submersible uses a mechanical arm.

Vocabulary in Context

EXERCISE

D. Choose the correct lettered response to define each numbered word or expression.

1. dates back to (¶ 1)
   a. has existed since
   b. has dwindled

2. intentional (¶ 1)
   a. potential
   b. planned and carried out

3. as of (¶ 1)
   a. at the time of
   b. like

4. extracting (¶ 1)
   a. taking out
   b. expanding

5. raw materials (¶ 1)
   a. manufactured substances
   b. natural resources

6. trenches (¶ 2)
   a. depressions
   b. mountains

7. wealth (¶ 3)
   a. large quantity
   b. lack

8. offshore (¶ 3)
   a. underwater
   b. current

9. immensity (¶ 3)
   a. feasibility
   b. large size

10. hydrostatic (¶ 4)
    a. alternate
    b. in water

11. crushing (¶ 4)
    a. capable of destruction
    b. very fast moving

12. differential (¶ 5)
    a. frequency
    b. difference in measurement

13. enormous (¶ 5)
    a. large
    b. small

14. consequences (¶ 5)
    a. effects
    b. adaptation

15. surfaces (¶ 5)
    a. ascends
    b. descends

16. shallow (¶ 5)
    a. not very deep
    b. sea-level

17. date from (¶ 6)
    a. have not been seen since
    b. first appeared in

18. depth capability (¶ 7)
    a. depth limit
    b. size

19. dexterity (¶ 7)
    a. weakness
    b. maneuverability

20. free (¶ 8)
    a. unpaid
    b. unattached

21. corresponding (¶ 8)
    a. opposite
    b. accompanying

COMPREHENSION SKILL INDEX — **Long Preposed Modifying Clusters**

Noun compounds and compound adjectives are very common in scientific and technical writing.

examples: laser beams

crop studies

earthquake prediction programs

petroleum-dependent system

high-level personnel

delta-winged aircraft

These forms are so prevalent in science writing that it is not unusual to find very lengthy examples—particularly ones containing numbers—many times within a single paragraph.

example: An eight-by-three-meter specially constructed solar panel was installed in the new office building.

Manganese nodules mined from the ocean floor
American Mining Congress Journal

Long Preposed Modifying Clusters

EXERCISE

E. The reading on pages 67-69 contains thirty long modifiers. The nouns and noun compounds they modify are listed below. In the space provided, give the complete phrase, including the noun (or noun compound) and all its preceding modifiers.

1. technology (¶ 1) _____

_____

2. depths (¶ 2) _____

_____

3. substances (¶ 3) _____

_____

4. supplies (¶ 3) _____

_____

5. yields (¶ 3) _____

_____

6. mining and retrieval (¶ 4) _____

_____

7. depth (¶ 4) _____

_____

8. force (¶ 4) _____

_____

9. technology (¶ 4) _____

_____

10. areas (¶ 5) _____

_____

11. area (¶ 5) _____

_____

12. one (¶ 5) _____

_____

13. pressure (¶ 5) _____

_____

14. pressure (¶ 5) _____

_____

15. depth (¶ 5) _____

_____

16. increase (¶ 5) _____

_____

17. technology (¶ 6) _____

_____

18. depth limit (¶ 6) _____

_____

19. sphere (¶ 6) _____

_____

20. conditions (¶ 6) _____

_____

21. submersibles (¶ 7) _____

_____

22. sphere (¶ 7) _____

_____

23. body (¶ 7) _____

_____

24. pressure (¶ 7) _____

_____

25. craft (¶ 7) _____

_____

26. cruising speed (¶ 7) _____

_____

27. arm (¶ 7) _____

_____

28. submersible (¶ 7) _____

_____

29. submersible (¶ 8) _____

_____

30. exploration (¶ 8) _____

_____

Etiology and Treatment of Essential Hypertension

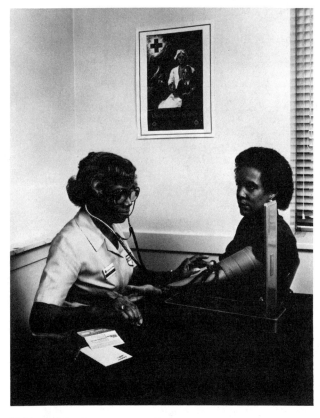

Taking a blood pressure reading

Subtechnical Vocabulary

mechanism (noun)

> causative factor; active part; instrument or process by which something is done
>
> The **mechanism** of cancer inhibition in shark blood is still unidentified.

output (noun)

> work performed; substance, energy, work, or power produced by some operation
>
> Industrial **output** can be increased by the intelligent use of robots.

deviation (noun)

> change from the expected course; abnormality
>
> An anomaly is a **deviation** from what is generally accepted as normal.

norm (noun)

> the average; the expected; the typical or normal for a particular group
>
> Since amaranth is a wild plant, there is no known **norm** for its harvest time.

workload (noun)

> amount of work to be performed
>
> The **workload** in engineering schools is very heavy.

a heavy workload

modality (noun)

> means; type; method
>
> There are several **modalities** of backache treatment: exercise, surgery, and anti-inflammatory drugs.

measure (noun)

    action taken to accomplish a goal

    Decompression is an essential safety **measure** taken by divers in their ascent.

relief (noun)

    lessening or stopping of pain or suffering

    He has had no **relief** from this pain since it began two weeks ago.

intake (noun)

    what is taken in or consumed

    Most doctors recommend an increased **intake** of fluids in the treatment of kidney infections.

a large intake of water

cessation (noun)

    stopping

    The **cessation** of brain wave activity is now what medically and legally defines death.

chronic (adjective)

    constant; continuing; permanent; recurrent

    Diabetes is usually a **chronic** disease; colds are not.

transient (adjective)

    of short, temporary, or momentary duration

    Certain drugs can cause **transient** side effects, such as sleepiness.

borderline (adjective)

    between two categories; between normal and abnormal; almost

    There is no such thing as **borderline** cancer—you either have it or you don't.

overload (noun)

quantity (of work) or something else above the possible; too much

An **overload** of clothing in an appliance such as an automatic washing machine will decrease its efficiency.

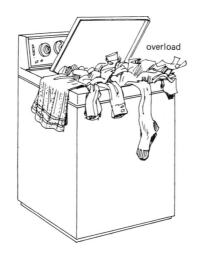

overload

intermittent (adjective)

stopping or starting periodically

In the tropical rainy season, there is **intermittent** rain all day.

to calibrate (verb)

to adjust and mark a measuring device in order to make it conform to a standard measure

Thermometers **are calibrated** in degrees Celsius or degrees Fahrenheit.

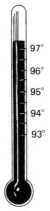

a Fahrenheit thermometer

to compensate [for] (verb)

> to make up for; to counterbalance a deviation from the norm

> It is difficult for the body **to compensate** for a period of malnutrition.

to fluctuate (verb)

> to change repeatedly from one position to another; to vary irregularly

> In this city the summer temperatures are a fairly constant 20°C; they **don't fluctuate** very much.

to range (verb)

> to extend from one particular quantity or point to another; to fluctuate within specific limits

> Temperatures in that other city, on the other hand, **range** from 18°C to 24°C from day to day.

to exhibit (verb)

> to show, particularly signs or symptoms

> Divers with the bends **exhibit** signs of pain, irritability, and nausea.

to block (verb)

> to prevent activity of; to obstruct or prevent entrance

> The danger posed by arterial plaque buildup is that the deposits **can block** the arteries.

blocking a door

to enhance (verb)

> to make stronger or larger; to increase (particularly some quality)

> Certain medications **enhance** the effect of others.

to indicate (verb)

> to be medically or otherwise necessary or strongly suggested

> Whenever there is a possibility that a bone might be broken, X-rays **are indicated**.

Vocabulary of Ideas

underlying (adjective)

> not immediately visible because of lying under something else; basic, fundamental

> The **underlying** causes of cancer are poorly understood.

consistently (adverb)

> in the same way; constantly; predictably

> This student is **consistently** finished with her work before the rest of the class.

significantly (adverb)

> to a great or considerable degree

> Alcohol **significantly** enhances the effect of certain sleeping medications.

A patient with the thyrotoxicosis of Graves Disease, one important cause of secondary hypertension

Courtesy Armed Forces Institute of Pathology, Washington, D.C.

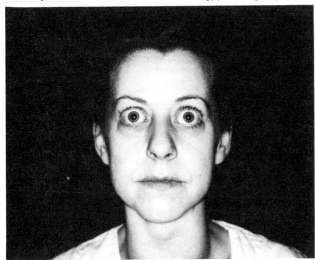

Thought Connectors

conversely | High blood pressure can cause kidney damage; **conversely**, kidney disease can cause high blood pressure.

regardless | **Regardless** of the possible consequences, I want to travel through space to another planet.

Vocabulary Exercises

A. Complete the following sentences with words from the list.

modalities | calibrated
cessation | compensate
blocked | workload
measures | norm
significantly | mechanism

1. Often a less intelligent student can _____ for his lack of ability by studying more.

2. The two most important _____ of cancer treatment are radiation and chemotherapy.

3. After exposure to certain infectious diseases, there are some

   _____ that may be taken to help prevent or lessen the disease.

4. Robots are capable of carrying a larger _____ than human workers because they do not get tired the way human workers do.

5. The acid rain problem can be _____ lessened if scrubbers are installed in industrial smokestacks.

6. The _____ of breathing does not necessarily indicate death.

7. A heart attack can occur when a coronary artery is _____.

8. All measurement instruments must be _____ to a standardized scale.

9. The _____ is that children stay with their parents until they are ready to support themselves on their own.

10. In the field of medicine, the factor that causes a disease is sometimes called its

    _____.

B. Choose the correct lettered response to complete each numbered statement.

1. The resting pulse rate of a healthy person should be fairly constant and not

   _____ very much.
   a. range
   b. calibrate
   c. fluctuate
   d. compensate

2. _____ of the underlying mechanism, heredity or environment, many disorders can be controlled, and many can be cured.
   a. Conversely
   b. Regardless
   c. Significantly
   d. Relief

3. The pregnant woman must increase her _____ of almost all nutrients.
   a. intake
   b. output
   c. cessation
   d. norm

4. Usually aspirin provides _____ of headache pain.
   a. modality
   b. measure
   c. output
   d. relief

5. It is the industrial _____ of sulfur in the combustion process that needs to be reduced.
   a. mechanism
   b. intake
   c. output
   d. workload

6. A(n) _____ disorder is one that lasts a long time and probably cannot be cured.
   a. chronic
   b. transient
   c. borderline
   d. intermittent

7. _____, many infectious diseases are transient and can be cured with proper treatment.
   a. Consistently
   b. Conversely
   c. Significantly
   d. Regardless

8. The pollution levels in this town do not fluctuate much; they are _____ below the danger level.
   a. consistently
   b. enhanced
   c. transiently
   d. conversely

9. The pH in this lake is _____ hazardous.
   a. borderline
   b. intermittent
   c. transient
   d. underlying

10. Knowing the harvest time of amaranth would _____ its value as a food crop.
    a. block
    b. calibrate
    c. fluctuate
    d. enhance

11. A(n) _____ of sugar can be harmful to the metabolism.
    a. overload
    b. measure
    c. deviation
    d. modality

12. Patients _____ symptoms of chest pain, shortness of breath, and dizziness should be carefully monitored.
    a. underlying
    b. exhibiting
    c. enhancing
    d. blocking

13. The scale of relative alkalinity and acidity _____ from 1 to 14.
    a. compensates
    b. ranges
    c. exhibits
    d. fluctuates

14. _____ periods of depression or anxiety could be a symptom of physical disease.
    a. Underlying
    b. Intermittent
    c. Borderline
    d. Calibrated

15. There are many diseases which are self-limiting and for which treatment is not

    _____.
    a. enhanced
    b. blocked
    c. calibrated
    d. indicated

16. _____ symptoms that occur intermittently can often be just as serious as chronic ones.
    a. Underlying
    b. Transient
    c. Borderline
    d. Indicated

17. Homosexuality is a _____ from the norm.
    a. deviation
    b. mechanism
    c. modality
    d. measure

18. It is not just what is in the topmost sediments that is important; often it is essential

    to examine the _____ strata if mineral deposits are to be found.
    a. underlying
    b. intermittent
    c. borderline
    d. chronic

An automatic blood pressure monitor measures systolic, diastolic, and mean arterial pressure.

Bard Biomedical

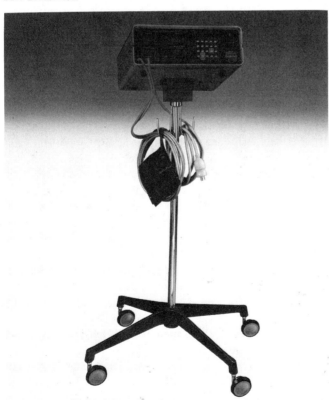

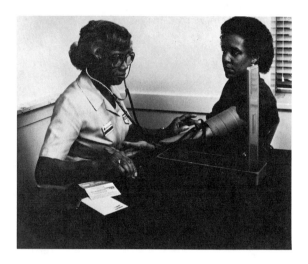

A blood pressure reading being taken with a sphygmomanometer

American Red Cross

Reading Selection

etiology: origin or cause

Etiology and Treatment of Essential Hypertension

Estimated to affect some 40 million people in North America alone, and more than 20 percent of the population worldwide, hypertension is the most common **chronic** disorder known. This often asymptomatic condition, in which the blood in the circulatory system exerts an elevated pressure against artery walls, results in reduced life span if left untreated. It has long been known that hypertensive patients die prematurely. Indeed, a directly proportional relationship between blood pressure and morbidity and mortality has been repeatedly demonstrated, and the higher the pressure, the worse the prognosis. **Conversely**, it has been shown that treatment **significantly** reduces morbidity and mortality.   1

morbidity: illness

prognosis: outlook

complex: set

idiopathic: of unknown cause

hormone: glandular secretion

contraceptive: birth control

thyrotoxicosis: overactivity of the thyroid gland

endocrine: glandular

Sufferers of this major symptom of a complex of diseases can be divided into two groups: those whose hypertension is variously labeled essential, primary, or idiopathic, and those whose high blood pressure is called secondary. Secondary hypertension has a known pathogenic factor, such as steroid, thyroid hormone, or oral   2 contraceptive use; severe kidney disease; thyrotoxicosis; certain tumors; and certain endocrine disturbances, among other factors. Essential hypertension, on the other hand, is a disorder of unknown etiology and accounts for a large (over 90 percent) majority of cases.

Blood pressure is measured with a sphygmomanometer, in which a scale **is calibrated** in millimeters of mercury (mmHg), and is expressed as a fraction in which the top number represents systolic pressure—or pressure when the heart contracts, forcing blood into circulation—and the bottom number represents diastolic pressure—or the pressure that exists in the circulatory system between heartbeats. The systolic pressure measures how hard the heart must pump to overcome arterial resistance. A reading of 135/85 mmHg indicates a systolic pressure of 135 mmHg and a diastolic pressure of 85 mmHg. Expected ranges for blood pressures have been established. These serve as standards against which an individual patient's readings can be compared and from which a diagnosis of hypertension can be made. The following are pressures above which a patient will generally be classified as hypertensive.

3

$$♀ \text{ any age} \geqslant 160/95$$

$$♂ \text{ above } 45 \geqslant 140/95$$

$$♂ \text{ below } 45 \geqslant 130/95$$

This chart, however, represents an oversimplification, since arterial pressure readings are known **to fluctuate** widely in all people at various times. Even the stress of a medical examination can elevate the blood pressure **transiently**. Ordinarily a normotensive patient is one in whom pressures are **consistently** lower than those on the chart; a sustained hypertensive patient is one in whom diastolic pressure always exceeds 105 mmHg; and a **borderline** hypertensive patient is one in whom diastolic pressures **range** from 90 or 95 to 105 mmHg or who **exhibits** an **intermittent** elevation of systolic and/or diastolic pressure.

4

sustained: consistently

The **underlying mechanism** of idiopathic blood pressure elevation is unknown, but excessive sodium ingestion, heredity, personality type, and environmental factors have all been implicated. Most theories suggest either a primary increase in peripheral resistance within the blood vessels or a deficiency in renal sodium **output**. These two theories are not necessarily mutually exclusive. For arterial pressure to rise, there must be an increase either in cardiac output (which would occur if the kidneys excreted less sodium than they should, thus leading to greater blood volume to be pumped) or an increase in peripheral resistance (possibly caused by plaque buildup), or both. Although it is known that arterial pressure is the product of cardiac output and peripheral resistance, the cause of the **deviation** from the **norm** remains largely unknown. **Regardless** of the primary initiating factor or factors, what is known is that the kidneys probably play a central role, possibly through a complex biochemical process involving the renin-angiotensin-aldosterone system.

5

renal: related to the kidney

cardiac: related to the heart

excreted: released, emitted

The effects of untreated hypertension can be lethal. The disorder forces the heart **to compensate** for the excessive **workload** imposed on it by increased arterial pressure. It is widely accepted that this condition is associated with a life span diminished on average by ten to twenty years, usually due to the increased rate of the atherosclerotic process. High blood pressure predisposes patients to debilitating and often fatal conditions, the major categories of which are heart disease, cerebrovascular accidents, and kidney failure. **6**

Certain risk factors associated with high blood pressure significantly **enhance** the effects of hypertension on mortality regardless of age, race, or sex. The most important of these risk factors are glucose intolerance, overweight, elevated cholesterol level, and cigarette smoking. These appear to have an additive effect. **7**

Therapy is indicated in all borderline and sustained hypertensives and may combine nondrug and drug **modalities.** Among the nondrug **measures** are **relief** of stress, improved diet, exercise, and control of other risk factors. Most clinicians recommend the restriction of sodium in the diet to a maximum of 5g NaCl per day; caloric restriction to control obesity; moderate reduction of cholesterol and saturated fat **intake;** and the **cessation** of cigarette smoking. Antihypertensive drugs are also prescribed when **indicated.** **8** These medicines, of which diuretics (for increased sodium excretion), antiadrenergic agents (for reduction of heart output), and vasodilators (for reduction of arterial resistance) play a large role, are individually or collectively the most commonly used drug therapies. The most promising are those antiadrenergic agents known as beta-blockers, because they are capable of **blocking** the sympathetic stimulation of the heart, thus decreasing its **overload.**

Although the complex root causes of hypertension are poorly understood, a significant reduction in morbidity and mortality has been achieved with treatment. Emphasis at present should be on **9** identifying patients who do not yet exhibit symptoms of long-standing hypertension and treating them before damage can occur.

Comprehension

EXERCISE

C. Choose the best lettered response to answer each question.

1. How many North American hypertensives are there?
   a. 40,000,000
   b. 40,000,000,000
   c. 4,000

2. What is the most frequent chronic disorder at present?
   a. high blood pressure
   b. anxiety
   c. the common cold

3. What happens when blood pressure is high?
   a. The blood only moves up the arteries, not down.
   b. The blood stops circulating.
   c. The blood pushes too hard against the arteries.

4. What is the major result of untreated hypertension?
   a. a shortened life
   b. weight loss
   c. immediate death

5. What increases with increased blood pressure?
   a. the rates of sickness and death
   b. the prognosis
   c. the repetition of demonstrations

6. What enhances the chances for a healthy and normal life span?
   a. treatment
   b. morbidity
   c. mortality

7. What are the two major categories into which hypertensives fall?
   a. essential and idiopathic
   b. morbidity and mortality
   c. primary and secondary

8. What do we know about the underlying mechanism of secondary hypertension?
   a. We know what it is.
   b. We don't know its etiology.
   c. We know it is a fatal condition.

9. Which of the following can cause secondary hypertension?
   a. severe kidney disease
   b. heredity
   c. overuse of the sphygmomanometer

10. What causes essential hypertension?
    a. We are not sure.
    b. a large number of cases
    c. thyrotoxicosis, among other factors

11. How is blood pressure measured?
    a. with a specialized instrument
    b. with a thermometer
    c. with a scale

12. How is blood pressure expressed?
    a. in strange behavior
    b. as an unknown etiology
    c. as systolic over diastolic pressure

13. Which pressure is higher, the systolic or the diastolic?
    a. the systolic
    b. the diastolic
    c. neither

14. What does diastolic pressure measure?
    a. the pressure between heartbeats
    b. the circulatory system
    c. the pressure when the heart beats

15. Which of the following blood pressures is too high?
    a. 110/70
    b. 115/80
    c. 170/95

16. What is characteristic of blood pressure?
    a. It does not remain constant.
    b. It does not change in some people.
    c. It is an oversimplification.

17. What factor might account for a temporarily abnormally high reading?
    a. fear during the time pressure is measured
    b. severe chronic kidney disease
    c. heredity

18. How does a normotensive patient differ from a borderline hypertensive?
    a. in the consistency of the normal readings
    b. in the underlying mechanism
    c. in the diastolic pressure

19. What are some possible causes of essential hypertension?
    a. idiopathic blood pressure elevation
    b. a known underlying mechanism
    c. diet, genetics, and personality type

20. What two factors are often named in most theories of blood pressure etiology?
    a. a decrease in sodium ingestion and an increase in resistance
    b. an increase in peripheral resistance and a deficiency in sodium excretion
    c. personality type and environment

21. What is known about the primary initiating factor in hypertension?
    a. The norm is unknown.
    b. It is lethal.
    c. The kidneys play an important part.

22. What does the heart have to compensate for in hypertension?
    a. fatal conditions, such as heart disease and cerebrovascular accidents
    b. increased atherosclerosis
    c. the excessive workload imposed on it by increased arterial pressure

23. What are some of the most dangerous risk factors to have with hypertension?
    a. overweight, high blood cholesterol, and cigarette smoking
    b. mortality and morbidity
    c. age, race, and sex

24. Which hypertensives should get treatment?
    a. modalities and measures
    b. normotensive and borderline
    c. borderline and sustained

25. Aside from sodium restriction, what other nondrug measures are recommended for hypertensives?
   a. a maximum of 5 grams of sodium per day
   b. diet, exercise, and relief of stress
   c. beta-blockers

26. Which are the most common of the drug therapies?
   a. diuretics, antiadrenergic agents, and beta-blockers
   b. diuretics, antiadrenergic agents, and vasodilators
   c. vasodilators

27. What do beta-blockers do?
   a. decrease cardiac overload
   b. stimulate the heart
   c. promise therapy

28. What has been accomplished with treatment?
   a. decreased illness and death
   b. the root causes
   c. longstanding hypertension

Drawing Conclusions

EXERCISE

D. Draw conclusions from the reading. Choose a or b to answer each question.

1. Why is the systolic pressure always higher than the diastolic pressure?
   a. because the blood exerts less force on the artery walls when the heart is not beating
   b. because certain blood vessels have more resistance than others

2. What is necessary in order to determine if a patient has sustained or borderline hypertension?
   a. one accurate reading
   b. repeated readings over a period of time

3. What conclusion can be drawn from the standard pressures shown between paragraphs 3 and 4?
   a. Women can withstand higher blood pressure than men.
   b. Blood pressures do not fluctuate much.

4. How could plaque buildup increase peripheral resistance?
   a. by narrowing the space the blood must travel through
   b. by increasing blood volume

5. What can you guess about the role of sodium?
   a. It causes friction in the blood vessels.
   b. It holds fluid in the body.

Vocabulary in Context

E. The first word in each group was used in the reading. Circle the word in each group which is closer in meaning to the first word.

1. disorder/syndrome/blood (¶ 1)
2. asymptomatic/harmless/silent (¶ 1)
3. prematurely/early/late (¶ 1)
4. pathogenic/causative/genetic (¶ 2)
5. ingestion/intake/workload (¶ 5)
6. implicated/blamed/caused (¶ 5)
7. mutually exclusive/very select/either-or (¶ 5)
8. product/result/cause (¶ 5)
9. peripheral/around the sides of the artery/in the kidney (¶ 5)
10. lethal/fatal/harmless (¶ 6)
11. predisposes/readies/inhibits (¶ 6)
12. additive/decreased in combination/mutually enhanced (¶ 7)
13. therapy/treatment/combination (¶ 8)
14. restriction/reduction/excretion (¶ 8)
15. prescribed/given/not permitted (¶ 8)
16. achieved/destroyed/accomplished (¶ 9)

COMPREHENSION SKILL INDEX

Adjective Clauses

Contributing to the density of scientific and technical writing is the frequent occurrence of the type of adjective clauses shown in the examples below. These sometimes seem difficult because of two factors: (1) the word order within the adjective clause, depending on the function of the relative pronoun; and (2) the insertion of the relative clause within the main clause, resulting in a discontinuous main clause.

examples: This is the book *in which I found the information I needed about hypertension.* (This is the book. I found the information about hypertension in it. I needed the information.)

It is often difficult to appreciate the factors *against which it is necessary to fight.*

A patient *in whom blood pressure easily rises with stress* may be a border-line hypertensive.

Note that these sentences truly condense two or more thoughts. They should cause no comprehension problems as long as you are able to identify the antecedent, you are aware of the various separate thoughts condensed, and you are familiar with this word order. In the first example you can see the three thoughts (given in parentheses). In the second and third examples, comprehension difficulties are caused by the word order within the adjective clause. Also, in the third example the adjective clause is inserted within the main clause rather than at the end of it.

Adjective Clauses

EXERCISE

E. Practice identifying the antecedent. For the following eleven adjective clauses taken from the reading on pages 86-88, write the antecedent in the space provided.

_____ 1. in which the blood in the circulatory system exerts an elevated pressure against artery walls

_____ 2. in which a scale is calibrated in millimeters of mercury (mmHg)

_____ 3. in which the top number represents systolic pressure—or pressure when the heart contracts, forcing blood into circulation—and the bottom number represents diastolic pressure—or the pressure that exists in the circulatory system between heartbeats

_____ 4. against which an individual patient's readings can be compared

_____ 5. from which a diagnosis of hypertension can be made

_____ 6. above which a patient will generally be classified as hypertensive

_____ 7. in whom pressures are consistently lower than those on the chart

_____ 8. in whom diastolic pressure always exceeds 105 mmHg

_____ 9. in whom diastolic pressures range from 90 or 95 to 105 mmHg

_____ 10. the major categories of which are heart disease, cerebrovascular accidents, and kidney failure

_____ 11. of which diuretics (for increased sodium excretion), antiadrenergic agents (for reduction of heart output) and vasodilators (for reduction of arterial resistance) play a large role

EXERCISE

F. Find each review vocabulary word in column a in the reading. Then choose a word or phrase from column b that may be substituted for the vocabulary word within the reading without any change in meaning.

a	b
1. artery (¶ 1)	tension buildup
2. results in (¶ 1)	deposits
3. exerts (¶ 1)	called
4. reduced (¶ 1)	makes up
5. directly proportional (¶ 1)	causative
6. mortality (¶ 1)	decreased
7. sufferers (¶ 2)	including
8. accounts for (¶ 2)	affected patients
9. to overcome (¶ 3)	measurements
10. readings (¶ 3)	causing
11. diagnosis (¶ 3)	causes
12. classified (¶ 3)	harm
13. stress (¶ 4)	of the surroundings
14. exceeds (¶ 4)	related as they vary
15. environmental (¶ 5)	identification of disease
16. suggest (¶ 5)	called
17. leading to (¶ 5)	blood vessel
18. buildup (¶ 5)	lead to the conclusion
19. initiating (¶ 5)	causing death
20. involving (¶ 5)	rates of death
21. is associated with (¶ 6)	pushes
22. diminished (¶ 6)	reduced
23. fatal (¶ 6)	counteract successfully
24. known as (¶ 8)	is higher than
25. damage (¶ 9)	is related to

Sunspots: A Potential Force in Determining World Climates

The Perkins Telescope at the Lowell Observatory in Flagstaff, Arizona (U.S.)

Subtechnical Vocabulary

shadow (noun)

> area darkened because it is blocked from the source of light by another object
>
> A **shadow** results when an opaque object stands in front of a light source.

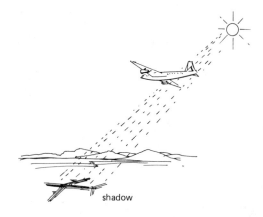

shadow

mass (noun)

> the measure of an object's resistance to acceleration
>
> The **mass** of a body is different from, but proportional to, its weight.

granule (noun)

> small particle; the smallest markings visible on the surface of the sun
>
> The **granules** on the surface of the sun can be seen through a telescope.

convection (noun)

> process of conveying; heat transfer between regions of unequal density caused by non-uniform heating
>
> **Convection** is a physical process that leads to a state of homogeneity.

buoyancy (noun)

> ability to float in a liquid or a gas
>
> The first necessary characteristic of a boat is **buoyancy**.

Wood is buoyant.

phenomenon (noun)

occurrence, particularly in science

Phenomena such as earthquakes show the amount of power nature has.

quiescence (noun)

inactivity

Most green plants have periods of growth alternating with periods of **quiescence**.

the naked eye

the eye, unhelped by any instrument to aid seeing

One-celled organisms are invisible to **the naked eye**.

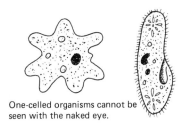

One-celled organisms cannot be seen with the naked eye.

to perceive (verb)

to see; to sense or feel

It is not easy **to perceive** slight differences in air temperature.

to arise (verb)

to originate; to come into being

It is not known if hypertension **arises** from any one specific cause.

to twist (verb)

to turn upon oneself or around something else; to form a coil

A rope that **has been twisted** appears shorter than a straight one.

to induce (verb)

to cause something to happen

It is not proved that excessive sodium ingestion **induces** hypertension.

to postulate (verb)

> to state as truth without proof; to form an idea or theory

> Scientists **postulate** that there must be something in the shark's blood that inhibits carcinogenesis.

postulating

rigid (adjective)

> hard; inflexible; not moving

> Concrete is a more **rigid** building material than wood.

Vocabulary of Ideas

to give rise to (phrasal verb)

> to cause

> High industrial sulfur emissions **give rise to** acid rain.

to rule out (phrasal verb)

> to eliminate as a possibility

> A diagnosis of cancer **does not rule out** the possibility of a normal life span.

to assume (verb)

> to conclude without evidence; to suppose

> Many people **assume** that if hypertension is asymptomatic, it must be harmless.

to coincide (verb)

> to occur at the same time as something else; to occupy the same space at the same time as something else

> This year the solar eclipse and the full moon **coincided.**

to maintain (verb)

> to insist; to hold to an argument or a theory

> The Chinese **maintain** that they have an accurate earthquake prediction system.

conjectural (adjective)

> a matter of opinion; involving guessing

> The future of robotics is largely **conjectural.**

predominantly (adverb)

> chiefly; mainly; most prevalently

> Acid rain is **predominantly** a hazard to aquatic life, although its effects are felt in other environments.

however (adverb)

> to whatever degree; regardless how

> **However** careful we are, accidents can still occur.

Vocabulary Exercises

A. Complete each sentence with a word or expression from the list.

assume	ruled out	buoyancy	the naked eye
rigid	twisting	phenomenon	mass
induced	shadow	granules	

1. A piece of metal lacks _____ in any body of water.

2. After preparing a wall for painting, _____ of paint and dust remain all over everything.

3. In an eclipse, the moon casts a _____ on the earth when it passes in front of the sun.

4. At night many planets and stars can be perceived with _____, while during the day a telescope is necessary.

5. The presence of radon in ground water before an earthquake is still an unexplained

   _____.

6. It is said that sharks can be _____ to attack by certain behavior, but there is very little evidence to prove this.

7. The possibility that some day amaranth will be a major food crop has not been

   _____.

8. Although we do not know for certain, we _____ that a diet low in saturated fats will result in a decreased risk of arterial plaque buildup.

9. The barn owl's eyes are stationary in their sockets, giving the owl's face a

   _____ appearance.

10. A coil is made by _____ some material such as rope or wire.

11. A measurement related to weight is _____.

B. Choose the correct lettered response to complete each numbered statement.

1. Because many complications can _____ during space flight, the crew aboard the spacecraft as well as the ground personnel must be well trained.
   a. maintain
   b. induce
   c. give rise
   d. arise

2. With the data transmitted from earth resource technology satellites, we can

   _____ areas of flooding and drought all over the globe in a very short time.
   a. perceive
   b. induce
   c. assume
   d. postulate

3. The designers of the one-person submersibles _____ that the newest models have all the maneuverability a free diver has.
   a. maintain
   b. give rise
   c. twist
   d. rule out

4. _____ certain we may be that we do not have hypertension, it is necessary to take readings to rule out the possibility.
   a. Predominantly
   b. Given rise to
   c. However
   d. Assuming

5. The matter of when laser arterial plaque removal operations will be available is still

_____; we will not know until we have seen sufficient animal data.
   a. rigid
   b. ruled out
   c. perceived
   d. conjectural

6. This fault is in a period of relative _____; there has not been an earthquake here for many years.
   a. quiescence
   b. buoyancy
   c. mass
   d. shadow

7. The scientific method involves _____ many theories and then investigating them fully either to prove them or to rule them out.
   a. twisting
   b. maintaining
   c. postulating
   d. perceiving

8. This year the astronomers' convention _____ with the first commercial space flight.
   a. coincided
   b. induced
   c. postulated
   d. maintained

9. Hypertension _____ many debilitating and even fatal disorders.
   a. perceives
   b. gives rise to
   c. maintains
   d. rules out

10. _____ occurs in both liquid and gaseous media.
   a. Quiescence
   b. Shadow
   c. Mass
   d. Convection

11. It used to be thought that arterial plaque buildup was _____ a disease of old age; now we know that even relatively young people suffer from it.
   a. conjecturally
   b. however
   c. predominantly
   d. rigidly

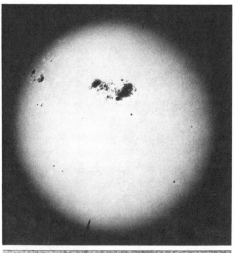

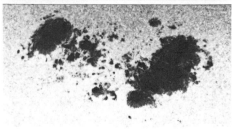

A whole disk and an enlarged view of an exceptionally large sunspot group

Hale Observatories

Reading Selection

Sunspots: A Potential Force in Determining World Climates

proximate: near

At a distance of about 150,000,000 kilometers, the sun is the earth's most proximate star. At over one hundred times the diameter of the earth, and at more than 300,000 times its **mass**, the sun's enormity is hard to imagine. Providing the light and heat on earth, this huge star is the generator and maintainer of all life and all life processes on this planet. Newly noted are indications that a solar activity known as sunspots **may have given rise to** certain historical occurrences. **1**

Appearing on the photosphere, the surface of the sun, and sometimes visible to **the naked eye**, are sunspots, dark patches known to exist for at least 2,000 years, although first scientifically studied in the seventeenth century by Galileo. It was, in fact, from studying the movement of sunspots that Galileo was able to conclude that the sun was a sphere rotating on its axis. With his telescope he **perceived** that the sunspots, which moved daily in a **2**

limb: outside margin

westerly direction, seemed to move at a slower rate near the limb than near the center of the sun.

Examined through a telescope, the sunspots are seen to have a dark center or **shadow**, the umbra, surrounded by a lighter area, the penumbra. All this appears superimposed on the **granulation** of the photosphere. The granules, which make up the photosphere, are the main **convection** mechanism of surface energy transport from the interior, hotter areas of the sun. Most recent theorists have suggested that sunspots **arise** from a complex physical process determined by the uneven nature of solar rotation. Unlike the earth, which rotates at a constant rate all over the globe, the sun, a gaseous rather than a **rigid** body, does not rotate uniformly. The equatorial regions rotate once every twenty-five days, while the polar regions take thirty-one days to complete one revolution. During this uneven rotation, magnetic lines of force get whipped up almost like cream being whipped in a bowl. Then centrifugal force, **buoyancy**, and turbulence further **twist** the lines of force and bring them to the surface, where they appear as sunspots.

3

Granulation visible on the solar surface

Hale Observatories

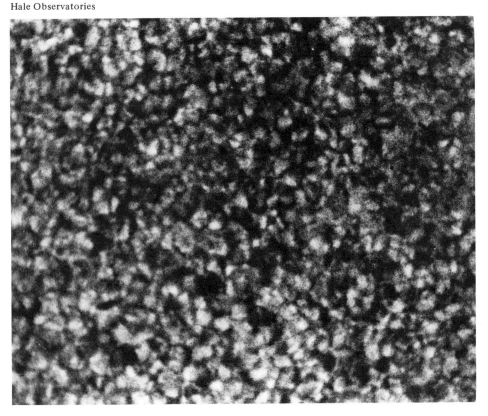

Magnetic field intensities of up to 4000 gauss have been recorded in the center of a sunspot. Often covering areas as large as the earth itself, these powerful magnetic fields are in many cases ten times the size of the earth. The sunspots typically produce temperatures of about 3500 K, which is significantly cooler than the average photosphere temperature of 5000 K. Very bright on their own, sunspots only appear to be dark against the photosphere because they are 30 percent as bright as the sun's surface.

4

Occurring mostly near the middle of the photosphere, sunspots are **predominantly** a **phenomenon** of the middle and low latitudes. The number of sunspots intermittently varies somewhat. At different times there may be as many as a hundred of them all at once, or none at all. The life span of smaller sunspots for the most part lasts less than a day, although larger ones may last a week or two and sometimes as long as a month.

5

Most interesting is the phenomenon of the 11.2-year average sunspot cycle. It is not known what causes this periodicity, although recent theorists have proposed some convincing arguments implicating Jupiter, with its 11.8-year solar rotation. It is suggested that this planet may be instrumental in **inducing** tidal action and sunspots.

6

Recorded also, however, are long periods of **quiescence,** the longest of which occurred over a seventy-five-year period in the seventeenth century. It should not, on the other hand, **be assumed** that this was the first—or even necessarily the longest—period of inactivity in history. Available to support the hypothesis of very long quiescent periods is isotopic carbon 14 evidence recorded in tree rings.

7

It has been noted that periods of sunspot quiescence **have coincided** with historically recorded periods of low temperature. **However** largely **conjectural** this hypothesis of direct correlation between solar activity and climate may be, it remains an attractive explanation for certain historical occurrences. One theory is that a long cold snap drove the Norse colony out of Greenland in the seventeenth century, thus ending Norwegian colonization of North America.

8

Another hypothesis is that, conversely, when the sun entered a long period of great activity during the twelfth century, it heated the earth, causing droughts. The drought in the southwestern part of the United States, it **is postulated,** may have driven the Pueblo Indians out of the Mesa Verde territory in Colorado. Although many climatologists **maintain** that more sufficient data need to be processed to confirm that there is any direct correlation between sunspot activity and terrestrial climate, the idea remains attractive to consider, and the possibility is difficult **to rule out.**

9

Comprehension

C. Mark the following statements T if they are true or F if they are false.

_____ 1. The sun is a star.

_____ 2. The sun is located 150,000,000 kilometers from the earth.

_____ 3. There are several stars at distances closer to the earth than 150,000,000 kilometers.

_____ 4. The sun is not as large as the earth.

_____ 5. Earth receives light and heat from the sun.

_____ 6. It has been known for a long time that sunspot activity caused many historical events.

_____ 7. The photosphere is a round photograph of the sun.

_____ 8. Sunspots can never be seen without a telescope.

_____ 9. Sunspots were first discovered in the seventeenth century.

_____ 10. Galileo has been known to exist for 2,000 years.

_____ 11. Sunspots appear to move when viewed through a telescope.

_____ 12. Galileo inferred the nature of the sun and the fact that it rotates.

_____ 13. Sunspots are made up of two areas, the umbra and the penumbra.

_____ 14. The photosphere appears granulated.

_____ 15. The granules bring energy from the interior to the surface of the sun.

_____ 16. The exterior of the sun is hotter than the interior of the sun.

_____ 17. The sun rotates in the same way as the earth.

_____ 18. The sun is made of gas.

_____ 19. It takes longer to rotate at the solar equator than it does to rotate at the polar regions.

_____ 20. Sunspots are actually magnetic fields.

_____ 21. Sunspots are hotter than the photosphere.

_____ 22. Sunspots are brighter than the surface of the sun.

_____ 23. The number of sunspots does not fluctuate much from one time to another.

_____ 24. Some sunspots die before the day is over.

_____ 25. The life span of a sunspot ranges from one day to about a month.

_____ 26. Sunspots last 11.2 years on average.

_____ 27. The cycle mechanism is well understood.

_____ 28. It is postulated that Jupiter may be responsible for sunspot periodicity.

_____ 29. Jupiter may induce the sunspots.

_____ 30. Sometimes there are long periods with no sunspots.

_____ 31. It is known that the seventy-five-year quiescent period that occurred in the seventeenth century was the longest ever.

_____ 32. Sunspot inactivity seems to be related to low terrestrial temperatures.

_____ 33. It is not known for sure if sunspots have a direct effect on climate.

_____ 34. It is possible that sunspot activity may have determined certain historical events.

COMPREHENSION SKILL INDEX

Distinguishing Fact from Theory

Certain words are used to indicate whether a statement is a fact or whether it is an opinion, a hypothesis, or a theory.

examples: Fact Indicators

be	Robots are entering industry.
confirm	These statistics confirm earlier suspicions that lung cancer incidence is increasing among women.
demonstrate	Experiments have demonstrated the effectiveness of the NMR.
determine	The cause of the fire has been determined.
establish	It has been established that space travel is feasible.
exhibit	These studies exhibit the correlation between acid rain and fish mortality.
know	We do not know the cause of essential hypertension.
prove	These results prove that reducing salt intake reduces blood pressure.
show	Experience with the NMR has shown that it is an effective and harmless diagnostic tool.
verify	The association between sulfur emissions and acid rain has been verified.
evidence	There is evidence that pollution of the world's oceans is on the increase.
fact	It is a fact that there have been fewer earthquakes here this year than there were last year.
proof	We have proof that some environmental factors can cause cancer.

Theory Indicators

appear	It appears that we won't be able to use robots as soon as we had hoped.
assume	We assume that salt consumption is related to blood pressure, but we do not yet have proof.
be + modals	It may be the cause.
believe	Many historians believe that sunspots are related to the occurrence of some world events.
guess	Some guess that arterial plaque vaporization will be available in a few years.
hypothesize	A few seismologists hypothesize that animals are able to "pre-sense" earthquakes.
maintain	They maintain that these animals are aware of minute tremors that cannot be felt by humans.
(modals)	We should know the results tomorrow.
postulate	Environmentalists have postulated a direct causal relation between water pollution and the extinction of certain species.
propose	The group proposes the following explanation for the connection between cancer treatment and lowered mortality.
reason	The reason that if scrubbers are installed, fish will be able to survive.
seem	The statistics seem to indicate that there is less heart disease in certain areas of the world than in others.
suggest	Studies have suggested that the bends can be prevented by slow decompression.
suppose	It is supposed that beta-blockers will become a more important treatment modality.
surmise	An association between heredity and certain diseases is strongly surmised.
suspect	Researchers suspect that viruses may be implicated in the etiology of diabetes.
theorize	Agronomists theorize that if its harvest time can be controlled, amaranth will soon be a crop in widespread use.
hypothesis	One hypothesis is that certain people are unlikely to get high blood pressure no matter what they eat.
idea	This idea has not yet been proved.
theory	It is a theory that is held by many researchers.

Other words, such as *infer, deduce,* and *indicate,* can be used as indicators of either fact or theory. Other context indicators will make it clear whether the author is stating a fact or a theory. As in all attempts at comprehension, however, context should be your final guide, as the words above are occasionally used paradoxically, incorrectly, or ambiguously.

Distinguishing Fact from Theory

EXERCISE

D. The following statements are either fact or theory. Look at the reading on pages 102-104 to find fact or theory indicators or evidence from the context to enable you to mark each statement *fact* or *theory*. Do not rely on your memory. Check the meaning of each statement in the reading.

_____ 1. Sunspots have given rise to certain historical occurrences.

_____ 2. Sunspots are dark patches on the photosphere.

_____ 3. Sunspots have existed for at least 2,000 years.

_____ 4. The sun rotates on its axis.

_____ 5. Sunspots move more slowly near the limb than near the center of the sun.

_____ 6. Sunspots are made up of two areas, a dark one and a light one.

_____ 7. The granules are a convection mechanism.

_____ 8. Sunspots arise from the uneven nature of solar rotation.

_____ 9. The sun does not rotate uniformly.

_____ 10. Magnetic field intensities of 4000 gauss have been recorded in sunspots.

_____ 11. Sunspots appear dark against the photosphere.

_____ 12. At different times there may be as many as a hundred of them, or none at all.

_____ 13. Jupiter causes sunspot periodicity.

_____ 14. Jupiter is instrumental in inducing tidal action and sunspots.

_____ 15. There have been long periods of quiescence in addition to the one recorded in the seventeenth century.

_____ 16. Sunspot quiescence has coincided with historically recorded periods of low temperature.

_____ 17. There is a direct correlation between solar activity and climate.

_____ 18. The cold drove the Norwegians out of Greenland in the seventeenth century.

_____ 19. The Norwegians left Greenland in the seventeenth century.

_____ 20. In the twelfth century there were droughts.

_____ 21. The Pueblo Indians left the Mesa Verde territory in Colorado.

_____ 22. The Pueblo Indians left the Mesa Verde territory in Colorado because of the drought.

Drawing Conclusions

EXERCISE

E. Choose a or b to answer each question.

1. How was Galileo able to reach the conclusion about solar rotation?
   a. because it was the only logical explanation for the apparent slowdown of sunspot movement near the limb
   b. because the sunspots did not move

2. In which direction does the sun rotate?
   a. from east to west
   b. from north to south

3. What reason would you give for the fact that sunspots occur mostly in the middle and low latitudes?
   a. buoyancy
   b. centrifugal force

COMPREHENSION SKILL INDEX

Uncommon Word Order

Unusual word order patterns used to vary writing style appear with high frequency in scientific and technical writing. If you are familiar with them, they will not interfere with your comprehension.

examples: Recently developed have been techniques for laser arterial plaque vaporization. (Instead of: Techniques for laser arterial plaque vaporization have been recently developed.)

New is the ability to scan the whole body with no X-ray radiation. (Instead of: The ability to scan the whole body with no X-ray radiation is new.)

Estimated to affect more than 40,000,000 North Americans, high blood pressure is the most common of the chronic disorders. (Instead of: High blood pressure is the most common of the chronic disorders and is estimated to affect more than 40,000,000 North Americans.)

In the first example the author begins the sentence with a past participle and a modifier that ordinarily would occur at the end of the sentence. Often such sentences begin with predicate adjectives. In the second example the author has moved the nonrestrictive adjective phrase to the beginning of the clause. It is important, as always, to find the noun phrase it modifies (this would ordinarily be called the antecedent—but not here, because it occurs after the adjective phrase, not before it).

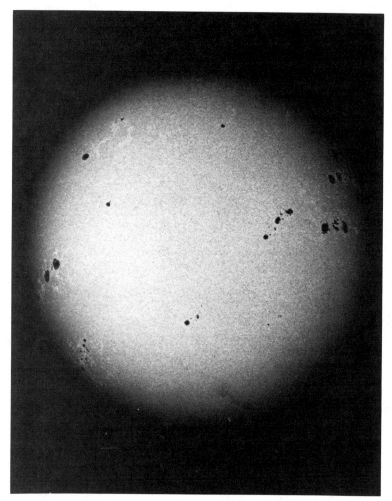

The surface of the sun with a large number of sunspots
Hale Observatories

Uncommon Word Order

EXERCISE

F. The following twelve examples using the uncommon word order patterns described above come from the reading on pages 102-104. In each sentence circle the noun or noun phrase described by the modifier.

1. At a distance of approximately 150,000,000 kilometers, the sun is the earth's most proximate star.

2. At over one hundred times the diameter of the earth, and at more than 300,000 times its mass, the sun's enormity is hard to imagine.

3. Providing the light and heat on earth, this huge star is the generator and maintainer of all life and all life processes on this planet.

4. Newly noted are indications that certain solar activity may have given rise to certain historical occurrences.

5. Appearing on the photosphere, the surface of the sun, and sometimes visible to the naked eye, are sunspots. . .

6. Examined through a telescope, the sunspots are seen to have a dark center or shadow, the umbra, surrounded by a lighter area, the penumbra.

7. Often covering areas as large as the earth itself, these powerful magnetic fields are in many cases ten times the size of the earth.

8. Very bright on their own, sunspots only appear dark against the photosphere because they are 30 percent as bright as the sun's surface.

9. Occurring mostly near the middle of the photosphere, sunspots are predominantly a phenomenon of the middle and low latitudes.

10. Most interesting is the phenomenon of the 11.2-year average sunspot cycle.

11. Recorded also, however, are long periods of quiescence, the longest of which occurred over a seventy-five-year period in the late seventeenth century.

12. Available to support the hypothesis of very long quiescent periods is isotopic carbon 14 evidence recorded in tree rings.

Polymer Batteries for On-Road Electric Vehicle Design

Studebaker No. 22b Electric Stanhope

A 1904 electric car

Subtechnical Vocabulary

mass produced (adjective)

manufactured in large numbers

The assembly line is the most widely used method in the manufacture of **mass-produced** items.

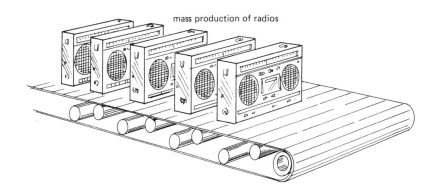

mass production of radios

marked (adjective)

significant; considerable; clearly defined

Acid rain has had a **marked** effect on the aquatic ecosystem.

theoretical (adjective)

lacking verification; based on speculation; unproved

The idea that sunspots have determined major world events is largely **theoretical**.

abundant (adjective)

numerous; plentiful; more than sufficient

It is hoped that photovoltaic cells will provide an **abundant** supply of energy in the near future.

inherent (adjective)

involved in the essential nature of something

Many problems are **inherent** in deep-sea diving.

short-lived (adjective)

of little duration; transient

Sunspots are relatively **short-lived** phenomena; most last only a day.

inert (adjective)

chemically or physically unreactive; exhibiting no chemical activity

Adding an **inert** substance does not affect the outcome of most chemical experiments.

electrode (noun)

collector or emitter of an electric charge; a device through which an electric current enters or leaves a medium

Batteries have positive and negative **electrodes**.

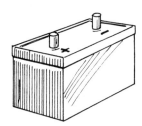

circuit (noun)

pathway through which electric current travels

Circuits are sometimes connected directly to a battery or other power source.

scarcity (noun)

relative lack; insufficient amount

There is a **scarcity** of natural resources in many areas of the world.

criterion (noun)

test on which a decision can be based or a judgment may be formed

The main **criteria** in determining the economic success of amaranth as a food crop are its hardiness and the predictability of its harvest time.

to outrank (verb)

to surpass in status or ability

The earthquake that occurred here last year **outranks** all others in the century in the amount of damage it caused.

to guard against (phrasal verb)

to work to prevent

Treating hypertension is one way **to guard against** strokes and coronary artery disease.

to immerse (verb)

to put under water; to cover with a liquid; to submerge

Certain metals can be cleaned by **immersing** them in acid.

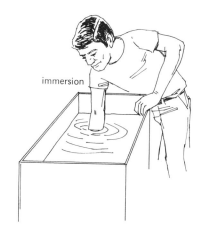

immersion

to dislodge (verb)

to remove from a previous attachment

The one-person submersibles are dexterous, yet they are strong enough **to dislodge** samples of mineral deposits on the ocean floor.

dislodging a stone

materially (adverb)

substantially; considerably; to a significant degree

The course of aquatic fish evolution could be **materially** altered by the acid rain problem.

Vocabulary of Ideas

to keep pace with (phrasal verb)

> to keep up with; to compete with successfully; to remain at the same level

> The development of alternative energy technology **has not kept pace with** the growing scarcityof fossil fuels.

to give way to (phrasal verb)

> to permit the other to win; to lose by choice or by passivity

> In recent years traditional eye surgery for retina reattachment **has given way to** laser repair of this disorder.

coupled with

> in addition to; joined with

> High salt consumption **coupled with** untreated hypertension can lead to very serious consequences.

in large measure (in large part) (expression)

> mainly; principally; largely; chiefly

> Many doctors believe that arterial plaque buildup is **in large part (in large measure)** due to a diet high in saturated fats coupled with a genetic predisposition to atherosclerosis.

at the outset

> at the beginning

> This professor admitted **at the outset** that even though he believed there was a cancer-inhibiting factor in shark blood, he didn't know if it would ever be identified.

in spite of the fact that

> even though

> **In spite of the fact that** we know what causes acid rain, we have done almost nothing to prevent it.

free (compound adjective-forming suffix)

> without

> In many respects, robots are more **trouble-free** than human workers.

Vocabulary Exercises

A. Mark the following statements T if they use the italicized word or expression correctly, or F if they use it incorrectly.

_____ 1. If you *keep pace with* other members of your class, you are a markedly better student than the others.

_____ 2. Eating a varied diet helps *guard against* nutritional deficiencies.

_____ 3. Objects in an art museum usually have been *mass produced.*

_____ 4. An *electrode* is a collector of electric current.

_____ 5. A *scarcity* is more than what is needed.

_____ 6. A *short-lived* phenomenon has a considerable life span.

_____ 7. A *criterion* is one factor used in a test or in helping form a judgment.

_____ 8. An *inert* substance is very chemically reactive.

_____ 9. The etiology of essential hypertension is *in large part* poorly understood.

_____ 10. A car that is *maintenance-free* is a gift from the mechanic.

B. Choose the correct lettered response to complete each numbered statement.

1. When you put something in a liquid you _____ it.
   a. dislodge
   b. immerse
   c. guard against
   d. keep pace with

2. Amaranth is a(n) _____ weed that needs hybridization in order to be exploited as a food crop.
   a. marked
   b. inherent
   c. abundant
   d. inert

3. It seems that the invasive diagnostic procedures are _____ the new scanners.
   a. giving way to
   b. keeping pace with
   c. guarding against
   d. in large measure

4. Electricity travels along a(n) _____.
   a. criterion
   b. scarcity
   c. electrode
   d. circuit

5. There is a _____ difference between electric trains and the maglev.
   a. marked
   b. short-lived
   c. dislodged
   d. mass-produced

6. Although many scientists believe arterial plaque buildup is largely caused by diet, this link is still _____.
   a. theoretical
   b. short-lived
   c. marked
   d. inherent

7. Dizziness _____ headache is a major symptom of the bends.
   a. given way to
   b. abundant
   c. guarded against
   d. coupled with

8. Untreated hypertension can _____ shorten life.
   a. at the outset
   b. materially
   c. theoretically
   d. in spite of the fact

9. Currently, gasoline-powered cars greatly _____ electric cars in number.
   a. outrank
   b. keep pace with
   c. guard against
   d. immerse

10. _____ sharks are not all ferocious, most people think they are.
   a. Inert
   b. Mass-produced
   c. Short-lived
   d. In spite of the fact that

11. It is difficult to _____ a piece of steel from a magnet.
   a. keep pace with
   b. guard against
   c. dislodge
   d. immerse

12. _____hypertension has no symptoms; but later it becomes apparent from a whole group of complications.
   a. In spite of the fact that
   b. At the outset
   c. Theoretical
   d. Inert

13. _____in any X-ray diagnosis is the danger of excessive radiation exposure.
   a. Inherent
   b. Theoretical
   c. Dislodged
   d. Immersed

A "hybrid" car combines both an electric motor and a gasoline engine under the hood.

Courtesy General Electric Research and Development Center

A prototype of an experimental, fully electric car
Courtesy General Electric Research and Development Center

Reading Selection

Polymer Batteries for On-Road Electric Vehicle Design

The significant cost advantage in a fuel-short world, **coupled with** the potential for **materially** reducing air pollution, has led to renewed interest in electric car development. Even though trucks, vans, and forklifts, among other electrically powered off-road vehicles, have been available and in operation for some time, development of a commercially acceptable, **mass-produced** electric passenger car **has not kept pace with** other technical developments in the auto industry. This is **in large measure** due to problems **inherent** in batteries as we now know them. It should be noted **at the outset** that electric cars are popularly regarded as anachronisms and museum pieces, **in spite of the fact that** at one time early in automotive history, they **outranked** gasoline-powered cars in widespread use. One day they may eventually recoup that position, and most drivers can expect to have driven an electric car before the century is up.

Interest in the traditional lead-acid battery has in recent years **given way to** more innovative power sources, in large part because of the **marked** disadvantages of the lead-acid storage battery, which

forklifts: factory machines for lifting heavy objects

1

have been appreciated for some time. There is, in fact, no inherent reason why lead-acid batteries have to be used in electric vehicles. Some of the exciting new batteries include a zinc-nickel battery, a zinc-chloride battery, a sodium-sulfur battery, and a lithium battery. Inherent in some of these newer batteries, however—several of which are still in the experimental stage—are problems of exceptionally high heat production (particularly in the sodium-sulfur and the lithium types), size and weight, and the necessity of **guarding against** chlorine gas release in the zinc-chloride battery. These batteries do, on the other hand, have the advantage of extremely high energy densities, ranging from 70 watt-hours per kilogram (which is double that of the lead-acid battery) to a **theoretical** 830-watt-hours-per-kilogram energy density. These high energy densities will enable electric cars to be driven much longer distances before needing a charge. **2**

What may now be the first important step in the mass production of electric automobiles is the development of a conductive polymer battery made of a material that is structurally similar to plastic but which has a metallic appearance and the ability to conduct electricity as well as lead does. This new plastic battery delivers twice as much power as the ordinary car battery, weighs less than 5 kilograms, and is virtually **maintenance-free**. It has the capacity to be molded into any shape, enabling it to be placed anywhere in the car, including under the roof, behind the door panels, or even beneath the seat. **3**

The conductive polymer battery is unlike the familiar lead-acid storage battery used in gasoline-powered automobiles. To review, the latter has two **electrodes** (one composed of lead [Pb], the other of lead dioxide [PbO_2]) which **are immersed** in an electrolyte—in this case, a solution of diluted sulfuric acid (H_2SO_4). Electricity is produced from the chemical reaction of these materials. A current of electrons flows from the negative terminal (lead), passes through an external **circuit**, and returns to the positive terminal (lead dioxide). The reaction can be shown as $PbO_2 + Pb + 2H_2SO_4 \rightarrow 2PbSO_4 + 2H_2O$. Simply stated, the chemical reaction of the battery creates an **abundant** supply of electrons at the negative terminal **4** and a **scarcity** of electrons at the positive terminal. However, over a period of time, the materials in the battery are used up and the battery goes dead. The battery then has to be recharged by plugging it into a battery charger which is subsequently plugged into an electrical outlet. The battery charger forces electrons through the battery in the opposite direction, reversing the chemical action, which restores most of the metal in the battery to its original form. But every time a battery is recharged, it loses some of its ability to produce electric current, and in time will need to be replaced. Most engineers believe the lead-acid battery is too heavy, too costly, and

release: emission

latter: last one mentioned, i.e., lead-acid battery

diluted: made weaker, usually by adding water

subsequently: next; later

too **short-lived** to play a major role in the development of electric vehicles.

Several types of conductive polymers are ready to be tested. One type is polyacetylene $(CH)_x$—(where x is some large but unknown number), a plastic made by linking acetylene molecules into long chains. Since polyacetylene is a natural insulator, it has no free electrons such as those in lead to move from atom to atom. The electrons in polyacetylene are all engaged in the bonding of atoms, leaving no free electrons to circulate about the molecule. To liberate the electrons, therefore, chemists dope the polyacetylene with chemicals such as iodine. Doping with iodine compound oxidizes the polyacetylene, **dislodging** an electron from one of its double bonds and causing it to attach itself to the iodine atom. Now the polymer becomes positively charged where the electron used to be, and the iodine becomes negatively charged. One researcher has tested several battery cells, one of which includes a piece of polyacetylene as a positive electrode and lithium metal as a negative electrode, all immersed in an electrolyte solution. Other polymers to

5

Lead-acid battery pack for the hybrid car

Courtesy General Electric Research and Development Center

be tested include polypyrrole and polyphenylene. Engineers expect to have completed their basic research within the next few years.

Besides its capacity to be molded, the plastic battery has several other advantages. In the lab the plastic battery can go through the charge-discharge cycle hundreds of times without permanently changing the polymer or the electrolyte. The polymers they are made of are relatively inexpensive. In fact, the material is so adaptable that it is being studied as a potential component of photovoltaic cells, long-distance transmission lines, and storage batteries for power stations. **6**

It is hoped that before long the product of this research will be a practical polymer conductive battery. Hurdles to overcome are the toxicity of dopants and the fact that many doped polymers lose their electrical characteristics upon exposure to air. It is widely accepted that the conductive polyacetylene must be kept in an **inert** atmosphere to prevent its immediate degradation. Polymer battery **7** research is important enough to have been given top priority by engineers and designers. This is because many researchers agree that if energy per unit weight and volume is the key **criterion** in battery success, the conductive polymer battery may be an important first step in electric vehicle development.

top priority: the most important place

Comprehension

EXERCISE

C. Insert *one* word taken from the reading in each of the following statements.

1. Two factors have contributed to the current renewed interest in

   _____ vehicles.

2. These two factors are air _____ reduction and fuel economy.

3. Some trucks, vans, and forklifts are non-gasoline-powered _____- road vehicles.

4. There has not been as much progress in electric passenger car development as there

   has been in the _____ industry as a whole.

5. _____ have many inherent problems which probably have been the cause of the relatively low level of interest in electric car development.

6. Even though electric cars were once in widespread use, they are now

   _____ by gasoline-powered cars.

7. Before the end of this _____, electric cars will be far more prevalent than they are today.

8. Most people think electric cars can only be seen in a _____.

9. There has been less _____ in lead-acid batteries recently.

10. We have known about the _____ of traditional car batteries for some time.

11. Some of the newer batteries, on the other hand, have _____ of their own.

12. Some of these experimental batteries generate too much _____.

13. The zinc-chloride battery may emit _____ gas into the air.

14. As in the lead-acid battery, _____ and large size need to be overcome.

15. One of the good things about the newer batteries is their high energy

_____.

16. Energy density is measured in watt-_____ per kilogram.

17. Because their energy densities are so high, it is possible to drive long

_____ without recharging them.

18. The most exciting of the experimental batteries is the _____ polymer battery.

19. The material used in this battery looks _____ but is structurally like plastic.

20. The polymer battery delivers double the _____ of the lead-acid battery.

21. This new battery requires almost no _____.

22. Its "moldability" gives designers the option of installing it

_____.

23. The _____ in the lead-acid battery are immersed in diluted sulfuric acid.

24. The chemical reaction within the battery produces _____.

25. The electrons flow from the _____ terminal to the lead dioxide terminal.

26. After a while the battery wears down and goes _____.

27. A battery charger reverses the _____ flow, restoring the metal to its original form.

28. Three of the problems inherent in the lead-acid battery are weight, cost, and duration of use, making it impractical for use in _____ cars.

29. Three polymers undergoing experimentation are polyacetylene,

_____, and polyphenylene.

30. Polyacetylene's electrons, unlike those in lead, do not move from atom to atom, but

rather are engaged in the _____ process.

31. The doping causes _____ of the electrons.

32. This is done by separating an _____ from its bond.

33. Soon the research will probably be _____.

34. _____ are poisonous.

35. Unless polyacetylene is kept in an _____ atmosphere, it
breaks down.

36. The key criterion in battery success is _____ per unit weight.

Vocabulary in Context

EXERCISE

D. Choose the correct lettered response to explain each numbered word or expression.

1. regarded as (¶ 1)
   a. considered to be
   b. looked at carefully

2. anachronisms (¶ 1)
   a. very new items
   b. items out of their proper time

3. recoup (¶ 1)
   a. recover or regain
   b. lose

4. charge (¶ 2)
   a. renewal
   b. change

5. delivers (¶ 3)
   a. needs
   b. provides

6. molded (¶ 3)
   a. shaped
   b. deteriorated

7. plugging into (¶ 4)
   a. striking
   b. connecting to

8. restores (¶ 4)
   a. buys
   b. replaces

9. insulator (¶ 5)
   a. something that does not permit passage of electricity
   b. electrolyte

10. practical (¶ 7)
    a. prototype
    b. feasible

Passive Infinitives, Perfect Infinitives, Perfect-Passive Infinitives

The simple (present active) infinitive, formed with *to* plus the simple form of the verb, is used in a variety of ways. Review some common uses of the infinitive.

examples: She wants *to identify* the cancer-inhibiting factor in shark blood.

There is nothing *to say.*

Is there something for me *to do?*

The goal of this program is *to reduce* air pollution.

Hypertension is too serious *to neglect.*

Amaranth is not yet predictable enough *to grow* commercially.

Some other uses of the infinitive can interfere with comprehension unless you are familiar with them. The passive infinitive, the perfect infinitive, and the perfect-passive infinitive are used often in scientific and technical writing because of the prevalence of reporting impersonally about recent developments. Sometimes the difficulty in understanding these uses of the infinitive is caused by the fact that they are made up of so many separate parts. At other times the problem may be the fact that the performer of the action is unclear. Whatever the reason, focusing attention on these uses of the infinitive should help you become familiar with them.

passive present
infinitive

examples: He didn't want *to be exposed* to radiation.

perfect infinitive

The tremors appear *to have ended.*

perfect-passive infinitive

It would have been impossible for sunspots *to have been discovered* until the invention of the telescope.

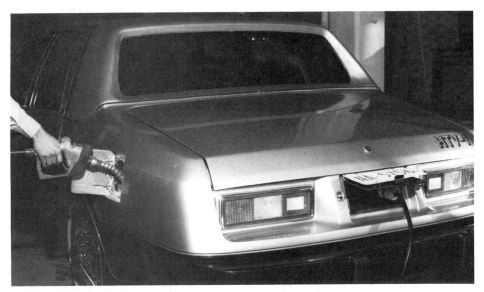

The hybrid car being refueled with both gasoline and electricity
Courtesy General Electric Research and Development Center

Passive Infinitives, Perfect Infinitives, Perfect-Passive Infinitives

EXERCISE

E. Demonstrate your understanding of the italicized infinitive forms. Choose the lettered response closer in meaning to each numbered statement taken from the reading on pages 120-123.

1. Most drivers can expect *to have driven* an electric car before the century is up.
   a. An electric car driven before the end of the century is most drivers' expectation.
   b. Before the end of the century, electric cars will be in widespread use.

2. There is, in fact, no reason why lead-acid batteries have *to be used* in electric vehicles.
   a. Use of the lead-acid battery is not a necessity in electric vehicles.
   b. We don't have lead-acid batteries to be used in electric vehicles.

3. These high energy densities will enable electric cars *to be driven* much longer distances before needing a charge.
   a. Before being driven, they will enable the high energy densities to be powered at no charge.
   b. Electric cars using batteries with high energy densities will drive longer distances between charges.

4-5. It has the capacity *to be molded* into any shape, enabling it *to be placed* anywhere in the car, including under the roof, behind the door panels, or even beneath the seat.
   a. Anywhere in the car can be molded.
   b. Its capacity to be molded makes it possible for it to be placed anywhere in the car.

6. The battery then has *to be recharged* by plugging it into a battery charger which subsequently is plugged into an electrical outlet.
   a. The electrical outlet is subsequently recharged by the battery plugged into the battery charger.
   b. First the battery is plugged into a battery charger, then the charger is plugged into an electrical outlet.

7. But every time a battery is recharged, it loses some of its ability to produce electric current, and in time will need *to be replaced.*
   a. The frequently recharged battery will wear out, and we will have to replace it.
   b. Every time a battery is replaced, it loses some of its electric-current producing ability.

8. Several types of conductive polymers are ready *to be tested.*
   a. Several types of conductive polymers have already been tested.
   b. Testing is ready to begin on several types of conductive polymers.

9. Engineers expect *to have completed* their basic research within the next few years.
   a. After having completed their basic research, engineers are expected within the next few years.
   b. Within the next few years, the basic research will be completed.

10. Polymer battery research is important enough *to have been given* top priority by engineers and designers.
   a. Engineers and designers have been given top priority in polymer battery research.
   b. Engineers and designers consider polymer battery research to be extremely important.

Improving Combustion Efficiency With FBC Technology

An industrial smokestack emitting polluted smoke into the air

Subtechnical Vocabulary

furnace (noun)

> enclosed space where heat is produced by combustion of fuel
>
> In the cold areas of the world, many residential buildings have their own **furnaces**.

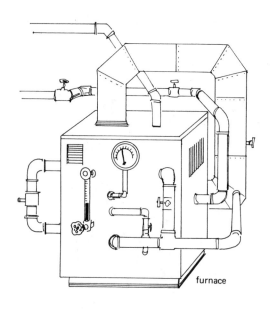

furnace

bed (noun)

> an ore deposit, usually horizontal
>
> An ore **bed** is usually parallel to the other rock layers of the area.

release (noun)

> liberation; emission

> The **release** of sulfur from industrial smokestacks is a serious environmental problem.

ignition (noun)

> burning; temperature at which burning begins to occur

> **Ignition** occurs when a fuel reaches a certain temperature.

demand (noun)

> need, especially an urgent need

> The body's **demand** for oxygen increases with strenuous exercise.

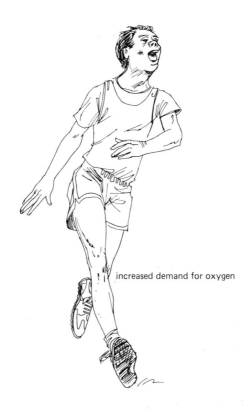

increased demand for oxygen

variable (noun)

> factor; characteristic that may change to affect a process

> There are probably several **variables** at work in the causation of hypertension.

corrosion (noun)

> breakdown or dissolving of metals, usually by chemical means
>
> Acids, when applied to many metals, are agents of **corrosion**.

byproduct (noun)

> substance produced by the production process of something else
>
> Carbon dioxide is a **byproduct** of respiration.

array (noun)

> selection of several alternatives; multitude
>
> There is an **array** of treatment modalities for mental disorders.

readout (noun)

> reading, particularly one recorded on paper or on a screen, often of computer data
>
> The **readout** indicates that temperatures have fluctuated for the last six months.

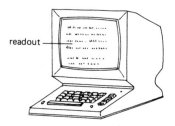

grate (noun)

> open metal platform, often used to hold fuel in a furnace
>
> A **grate** can only be used to hold solid fuel.

exothermic (adjective)

> heat producing or releasing
>
> Combustion is an **exothermic** process.

superfluous (adjective)

> more than is sufficient or necessary
>
> Consuming **superfluous** calories causes overweight.

to smolder (verb)

> to burn, but with no flame
>
> Burning charcoal does not go out abruptly; it **can smolder** for hours.

to trap (verb)

> to capture; to collect by closing off

> A filter **can trap** large particles in water.

to extract (verb)

> to remove or take out

> The broken tooth could not be repaired; it **had to be extracted**.

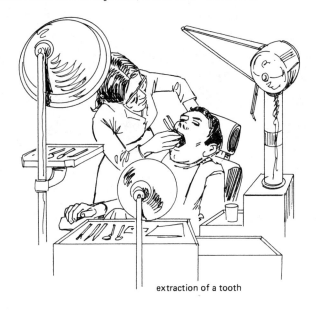

extraction of a tooth

to disperse (verb)

> to distribute over a large area

> Plant pollen **disperses** seeds in the direction the wind is blowing.

dispersion of seeds

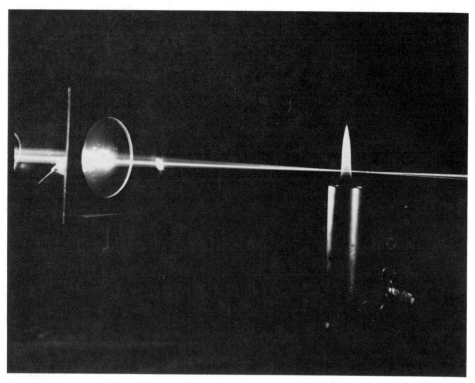

Lasers being used in combustion analysis
Courtesy United Technologies Research Center

to give off (phrasal verb)

> to emit; to release

> Heat **is given off** in an exothermic reaction.

to feed into (phrasal verb)

> to insert or put into someting

> Data **is fed into** the computer, where it is processed.

Vocabulary of Ideas

focus (noun)

> main interest; center of activity

> The **focus** of our study is improving fuel efficiency.

additionally (adverb)

    also

    Diabetes can be treated with insulin; **additionally**, it can be treated with diet and exercise.

fully (adverb)

    at least

    Fully 80 percent of the people in this town have been exposed to radiation.

as evidenced by

    as proved by; as indicated by

    We know that cutting down on sodium ingestion can lower the need for diuretics, **as evidenced by** the lowering of blood pressure readings from this dietary measure alone.

to entail (verb)

    to involve

    Successful space flight **entails** the simultaneous monitoring of numerous variables.

Vocabulary Exercises

A. Choose the best lettered synonym for the italicized word or expression in each numbered statement.

1. There is a *group* of instruments on the laboratory table. Do you know which one to use?
   a. readout
   b. array
   c. demand
   d. corrosion

2. Fuel can be *put* into this furnace through the pipe on the left.
   a. fed
   b. evidenced
   c. trapped
   d. extracted

3. Large air masses *scatter* pollutants over great distances.
   a. give off
   b. disperse
   c. extract
   d. trap

4. *At least* one-third of patients treated with antithyroid medication do not have problems with their thyroid glands again.
   a. Fed into
   b. As evidenced by
   c. Fully
   d. Additionally

5. In fossil fuel combustion, sulfur is one of the *substances created.*
   a. ignitions
   b. byproducts
   c. array
   d. furnaces

6. Useful substances can often be *removed* from waste.
   a. extracted
   b. trapped
   c. fed into
   d. evidenced

7. This professor is an expert in seismology; she is *also* a Nobel laureate in physics.
   a. fully
   b. additionally
   c. evidenced by
   d. superfluously

8. An *interest* of cardiology is noninvasive arterial plaque removal procedures.
   a. grate
   b. focus
   c. demand
   d. variable

9. Too high humidity can be instrumental in the *breakdown* of metals.
   a. release
   b. demand
   c. focus
   d. corrosion

10. The *need* for alternative power sources is urgent.
    a. demand
    b. array
    c. furnace
    d. ignition

11. What is *involved* in making amaranth economically feasible?
    a. given off
    b. evidenced
    c. dispersed
    d. entailed

B. Complete each statement with a word or expression defined at the beginning of the lesson.

1. The new computers are so fast they give a _____ in a fraction of the time it used to take.

2. The focus of recent furnace technology has been on _____ noxious particulates so that they will not be released into the air.

3. There must have been _____ if there is fire.

4. Harvest time is still a poorly understood _____ affecting amaranth cultivation potential.

5. The potential _____ of radiation into the atmosphere is one of the hazards of nuclear power plants.

6. The wood is slightly damp, causing it to _____ without really making a fire.

7. The iron ore _____ in the Mesabi Range are some of the largest in the world.

8. Smoke is _____ by fire.

9. Salt must be a factor in moderate hypertension _____ the fact that decreasing its consumption virtually always reduces pressure.

10. An _____ process is a heat-releasing process.

11. A _____ is a place to burn fuel for heating.

12. Many books are filled with _____ information that the reader doesn't need or want to know about.

13. The _____ of this lesson will be boiler and furnace technology.

A conventional gas boiler
Courtesy Weil-McLain

An FBC boiler

Lancaster Steel Co., Inc.

Reading Selection

Improving Combustion Efficiency With FBC Technology

Although it is not widely appreciated, combustion, an **exo-thermic** chemical combination of oxygen with the combustible elements of fuel, can occur with or without fire. The heat **given off** by combustion is the heat liberated by burning a unit mass or unit volume of fuel such as petroleum, natural gas, or coal. Extremely rapid combustion is called, simply, an explosion; however, combustion is not necessarily a rapid process, **as evidenced by** the **smoldering,** without fire, of underground coal beds for hundreds of years.

Efficient combustion **entails** maximizing the **release** of heat while minimizing losses from fuel imperfections and **superfluous** air. The three **variables** necessary to and determining the efficiency of the combustion process are temperature, time, and turbulence. First,

1

a sufficiently high temperature is needed to ensure the **ignition** of the constituents. Second, sufficient time is needed for complete combustion; and third, turbulence is needed for the mixing of the fuel with air. Although the fundamental physical laws applying to combustion, namely the Law of Conservation of Energy, the Law of Conservation of Matter, the Law of Combining Weights, and Dalton's, Amargat's, and Avogadro's Laws, have been understood for some time, the **focus** of recent combustion technology research has been on facilitating more efficient fossil fuel combustion through a deeper understanding of the process itself.

Instrumental in inducing this renewed interest in the basics of combustion is the fact that more than 95 percent the energy **demand** of the industrial world is met by burning fossil fuels. However, as the energy demand continues to rise, so does the fuel pollution rate. Of the three major combustible elements (carbon, hydrogen, and sulfur), only carbon and hydrogen are of importance as heat sources. Sulfur, on the other hand, is of importance because of its role as a polluter and in **corrosion**. Some of the unwelcome **byproducts** of burning fuel are sulfur and nitrogen oxides, which are emitted into the air by fuel-burning smokestacks and which form photochemical smog and acid rain.

An **array** of high-technology combustion analysis devices has recently become available. Among these are high-speed cameras and computers to probe and assess amounts of chemical materials produced in the combustion process. In the lab, fuel products burned at one-tenth normal atmospheric pressure allow a 3-millimeter flame to be stretched to 30 millimeters. A thermocouple passed through the enlarged flame provides observers with temperature **readouts** in various sections of the flame. Samples of the flame **can additionally be fed into** a mass spectrometer to identify the particulates in the chemical content of the flame. Another new procedure, known as Coherent AntiStokes Raman Spectroscopy (CARS), allows technicians to fire two laser beams of the same frequency into a flame, where they interact with it and produce light of another frequency, which is in turn analyzed for molecule differentiation and temperature measurement. This can be carried out even within the fiery innards of an operating jet engine or a furnace.

New is a method of fuel burning known as FBC, which stands for fluidized bed combustion. Tests have shown FBC boilers able to burn anything from sawdust and logs to oil shale and coal. Capable of controlling the noxious oxides of nitrogen and sulfur without the use of smokestacks **to disperse** the flue gases, or scrubbers **to trap** particulates, an FBC boiler is so efficient that it can operate at a temperature several hundred degrees cooler than conventional **furnaces** or boilers do. With the lower temperature, little nitrogen in the air inside the furnace or boiler is available to combine with

sawdust: wood particles

logs: long cylinders of wood, usually the cut trunk of a tree

oil shale: sedimentary rock containing oil

2

3

4

5

oxygen to produce nitrogen oxide. When the FBC burns fuels with a high sulfur content, crushed limestone or dolomite is fed into the boiler along with the fuel. There the sulfur in the fuel combines with the calcium in the limestone or dolomite to form calcium sulfite. Finally, this substance can be trapped inside the furnace from which it **is** finally **extracted** as ash. Studies have shown that an FBC unit can capture close to 90 percent of the sulfur in the fuel.

Applying the three t's of combustion (time, temperature, and turbulence), the FBC boiler works in the following way. First, fine sand is inserted into the FBC boiler on a **grate** or **bed**. Air is then blown into the grate, lifting and churning the sand particles and making them appear to "boil." To ignite the fire, propane is used until the sand particles reach red-hot temperatures of about 450°C, at which point the combustion process is self-sustaining. Then the gas is turned off and a fuel such as coal is added to the sand. The   6 coal will eventually be dispersed throughout the churning sand. With the addition of the fuel, the temperature of the bed reaches about 750°C. In an operating furnace water can be pumped through pipes running in and around the hot bed, producing steam to run an electricity-producing generator. In this operation tests have shown that water collects **fully** five times faster than piped water in a conventional boiler.

FBC units are currently being built in several countries to burn all kinds of fuels to produce heat and electricity. However, one of the main goals for FBC designers remains to develop and install   7 home furnaces that would be smaller and less costly and that would burn fuels more efficiently than the present conventional models.

Comprehension

EXERCISE

C. Mark the following statements T if they are true or F if they are false.

_____ 1. Most people understand that fire is not an inherent feature of combustion.

_____ 2. Combustion does not necessarily give off heat.

_____ 3. Oxygen is a factor in combustion.

_____ 4. Fuel is not necessary for combustion.

_____ 5. Petroleum, natural gas, and coal are inert substances.

_____ 6. An explosion is one kind of combustion.

_____ 7. Combustion is always short-lived.

_____ 8. One thing that proves that combustion can be long-lived is coal bed combustion activity.

_____ 9. Fuel constituents will ignite at any temperature.

_____ 10. Time is of no importance in combustion.

_____ 11. Turbulence is an unwelcome side effect of air and fuel mixing.

_____ 12. Unmoving air mixes best with fuel.

_____ 13. The fundamental laws applicable to combustion are only recently appreciated.

_____ 14. More research is needed on Dalton's, Amargat's, and Avogadro's Laws.

_____ 15. The goal of today's researchers is increased fossil fuel combustion efficiency.

_____ 16. The Law of Combining Weights is related to combustion.

_____ 17. The nature of combustion has been entirely understood for some time.

_____ 18. The process itself still needs some research if it is to be made more efficient.

_____ 19. In spite of the fact that more than 95 percent of the energy demand of the industrial world is met with fossil fuels, there is no interest in the combustion process.

_____ 20. Pollution increases in direct proportion to energy demand.

_____ 21. Carbon, hydrogen, and sulfur are combustible agents.

_____ 22. Sulfur is an important source of heat.

_____ 23. The unwelcome byproducts of industrial combustion are instrumental in photochemical smog formation and acid rain production.

_____ 24. Several new devices for studying combustion are available.

_____ 25. Scientists are interested in the chemical byproducts of combustion.

_____ 26. CARS is an acronym.

_____ 27. Lasers are used in studying flames.

_____ 28. CARS represents a breakthrough because it makes it possible to study the characteristics of flame in previously unreachable places.

_____ 29. Fluidized bed combustion is a new fuel-burning procedure.

_____ 30. FBC boilers are considerably more versatile than conventional boilers.

_____ 31. The nitrogen that forms nitrogen oxide is present in the air in the furnace.

_____ 32. Sulfur is an inert substance.

_____ 33. Propane is a kind of gas.

_____ 34. Sand particles are a fuel.

_____ 35. The sand moves.

_____ 36. One of the functions of a furnace can be to produce steam.

_____ 37. Electricity can be the final product of the combustion process.

_____ 38. FBC boilers are five times as efficient as conventional boilers.

_____ 39. FBC boilers have no potential use in residential buildings.

Vocabulary in Context

EXERCISE

D. Choose the correct lettered response to explain each numbered term or phrase.

1. unit mass or unit volume (¶ 1)
   a. a given amount
   b. a large amount
2. turbulence (¶ 2)
   a. movement
   b. engine
3. photochemical (¶ 3)
   a. related to pictures
   b. related to light
4. thermocouple (¶ 4)
   a. measures temperature
   b. measures connections
5. mass spectrometer (¶ 4)
   a. assesses size
   b. assesses content
6. differentiation (¶ 4)
   a. identification
   b. changing
7. fiery (¶ 4)
   a. wild
   b. hot

8. innards (¶ 4)
    a. interior
    b. propellers

9. boilers (¶ 5)
    a. furnaces
    b. fuels

10. churning (¶ 6)
    a. mixing
    b. burning

Drawing Conclusions

EXERCISE

E. Choose a or b to answer the following questions.

1. What is one proof that combustion doesn't always produce fire?
    a. the smoldering of coal beds
    b. extremely rapid combustion

2. What are some factors that adversely affect combustion efficiency?
    a. heat release and loss minimizing
    b. fuel imperfections and excess air

3. Why do scientists want to assess the amounts of chemical materials produced in the combustion process?
    a. so they can work towards reducing the emission of certain pollutants
    b. so they can take high-speed photographs of them

4. What is the effect of reducing atmospheric pressure?
    a. proportionally reducing the pollution rate
    b. proportionally increasing the size of the flame

5. What conclusion can you draw about the temperature of a flame?
    a. It is not uniform.
    b. It is uniform.

6. What is one feature of an efficient boiler?
    a. It disperses the flue gases.
    b. It operates at a lower temperature.

7. What is the specific effect of lowering boiler operating temperatures?
    a. It reduces nitrogen oxide production and therefore pollutes less.
    b. It burns fuels with a high sulfur content and therefore pollutes more.

Expressions of Sequence and Duration

Review the following expressions and words that are used to indicate sequence and duration. Although many of these expressions will not be new to you, they are included for the sake of completeness.

Sequence or Occurrence

after
After the current is shut off, the cell nuclei revert to their original positions.

after (a while, a time, some time, and so on)
After a while the current is turned back on.

after that
After that, the patient waits for the results.

afterwards
Afterwards there are no harmful side effects.

at once
The three reports arrived at once.

at one time
At one time it was believed that the world was flat.

at some time
At some time we will know how to predict earthquakes.

at that time
At that time we did not know how to recognize the warning signs.

at the outset (the beginning, the end, and so on)
At the outset it was not known that burning fossil fuels could result in so much fish mortality.

at the same time
These two fuels should not be burned at the same time.

before
Before planting a crop, you should know its probable harvest time.

before (some time, long, and so on)
Before long, FBC boilers will be available.

before (some time is up)
Before the month is up, we will know if this experiment was a success.

concurrently
You can take these two courses concurrently.

currently
Currently, FBC boilers are available for industrial use only.

earlier
The earthquake that occurred earlier was much stronger.

eventually
Eventually, many operations may be performed by lasers.

finally
Finally, after many years of animal experimentation, laser arterial plaque reduction is to be tried on humans.

first(ly) (second[ly] ... last[ly])
Firstly, FBC boilers can operate at lower temperatures.

formerly
Formerly it was thought that there would always be enough fossil fuel to serve our needs.

immediately
This must be fixed immediately.

in the future (the near future, the distant future)
In the future we will have to rely more on alternate energy sources.

later
Later it was learned that the earth rotates on its axis.

next

We now know what causes acid rain; next we will have to do something to prevent it.

now

Now we know that there is no one factor that causes high blood pressure.

one day (some day)

One day we may know how to prevent hypertension from occurring.

previously

Previously diabetes was a fatal illness.

recently

It has recently been learned that animals exhibit strange behavior before earthquakes.

simultaneously

New combustion technology permits technicians to measure flame size and temperature simultaneously.

subsequently

First it was thought that the sun was stationary; but subsequently it was discovered that it rotates on its axis in much the same way the earth does.

then

If we had known then what we know now, we would have taken some preventive measures.

ultimately

Ultimately we are going to see many more robots doing jobs formerly done by human workers.

upon

Upon seeing evidence of extreme stress build-up along the fault, local officials began to plan for potential disaster.

up until

Up until the twentieth century, maternal mortality was a significant factor in lowered life expectancy.

while

While the study is being carried out, it is better not to draw any conclusions.

Duration

before (some time) is up

Before the week is up, the new robots should be installed in this factory.

during (period of time)

During the implementation period, it is expected that there will be some friction between management and the factory workers.

for some time

It has been known for some time that reducing salt consumption lowers blood pressure.

from (specific time)

From today on, it is not permitted to burn fuels high in sulfur.

in (a year, a month, and so on)

It is impossible to master a language in two weeks.

in recent years

In recent years the acid rain problem has increased dramatically.

in time

In time all living things die.

over a period of time

Over a period of time, hypertensives can be expected to have more major illnesses than normotensives.

since (specific time)

Since the late 1880s antiseptics have been used routinely in surgery.

still

We still do not know what the cancer-inhibiting factor in shark blood is.

until

We will cultivate amaranth experimentally until our efforts are successful.

while

Almost no vibration is felt while the maglev is in operation.

within (period of time)

You should be able to take off one kilogram of body fat within a one-week period.

Expressions of Sequence and Duration

EXERCISES

F. Choose the lettered response closer in meaning to the italicized element in each of the numbered statements adapted from the reading on pages 138-140.

1. Even though electrically powered trucks, vans, and forklifts have been available and in operation *for some time*, development of a mass-produced electric passenger car has not kept pace with other technical developments in the auto industry.
   a. several times
   b. beginning in the past and continuing into the present

2. It should be noted *at the outset* that electric cars are considered to be anachronisms.
   a. on the outside
   b. first of all

3. *At one time* early in automotive history, electric cars were used more widely than gasoline-powered cars.
   a. concurrently
   b. in the past

4. *One day* electric cars will recoup their former position.
   a. at some uncertain time in the future
   b. suddenly

5. These newer batteries, some of which are *still* in the experimental stage, have problems that need to be overcome.
   a. unmoving
   b. yet

6. *Over a period of time*, the materials in the battery are used up and the battery goes dead.
   a. during an uncertain amount of time
   b. more than a period of time

7. Many doped polymers lose their electrical characteristics *upon* exposure to air.
   a. at the time of
   b. before

8. The battery charger is *subsequently* plugged into an electrical outlet.
   a. afterwards
   b. before

9. *Every time* a battery is recharged, it loses some of its ability to produce electric current.
   a. on each occasion
   b. forever

10. *In time* it will need to be replaced.
    a. at the right time
    b. eventually

11. Engineers expect to have completed their basic research *within the next few years.*
    a. during the next few years
    b. after the next few years have passed

G. Mark the following statements A if they refer to the present only or if they are time-less, B if they refer to the past only, C if they refer to the past and the present, D if they refer to the present and the future, or E if they refer to the future only. All sentences come from the reading in this lesson.

_____ 1. Some underground coal beds have been smoldering, without fire, for hundreds of years.

_____ 2. Efficient combustion entails maximizing the release of heat while minimizing losses from fuel imperfections and superfluous air.

_____ 3. The fundamental physical laws applying to combustion have been understood for some time.

_____ 4. An array of high-technology combustion analysis devices has recently become available.

_____ 5. This substance can finally be extracted as ash.

_____ 6. The coal is eventually dispersed throughout the churning sand.

_____ 7. FBC units are currently being built in several countries.

Vocabulary Review

EXERCISE

H. For each numbered term or expression below, find the review vocabulary word in the reading with the same meaning.

1. test for _____

2. material burned for power or heat _____

3. process of burning _____

4. given off _____

5. made larger _____

6. helpful _____

7. making it easier _____

8. known _____

9. put into use _____

10. at the present time _____

11. traditional _____

12. ray of light _____

13. put into _____

14. causing _____

15. accomplished _____

16. able to continue with no help _____

17. measure _____

18. permit _____

19. act together with _____

20. almost _____

21. types of appliances _____

22. harmful _____

23. small pieces _____

24. invent and manufacture _____

Growing Crops for the Future Through Bioengineering

A sunflower plant being inoculated with a gene-carrying substance in a genetic engineering project at the University of Wisconsin (U.S.)

Subtechnical Vocabulary

to boost (verb)

> to promote; to increase; to raise

> A good fertilizer **can** significantly **boost** crop yields.

to skip (verb)

> to omit or disregard

> Nutritionists say that breakfast is the most important meal of the day and **should** therefore **not be skipped**.

skipping breakfast

to mate (verb)

> to reproduce sexually; to pair for the purpose of breeding

> If you **mate** a horse and a donkey, the offspring will be a mule.

to isolate (verb)

> to keep alone or apart; to separate

> It is important **to isolate** patients with infectious diseases so that others will not become sick.

to apply (verb)

> to put onto; to use

> After a farmer plants seed, fertilizer **is applied** to the field.

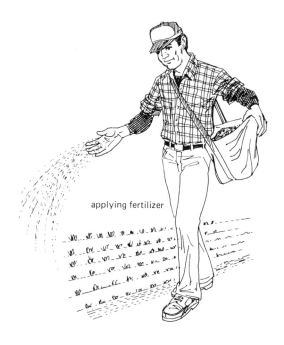

applying fertilizer

to stimulate (verb)

> to cause activity by some action; to excite

> Certain minerals **stimulate** plant growth.

to retain (verb)

> to hold; to keep

> A person with poor kidney function often has trouble excreting excess fluids and **retains** them in the body.

to splice (verb)

> to attach or join separate but like things

> Wire **can be spliced** at the ends.

to derive (verb)

> to originate; to come from

> Salt **can be derived** from the evaporation of sea water.

to pass along (phrasal verb)

    to cause (a trait) to appear through genetic inheritance

    Hemophilia is a sex-linked trait; it **is passed along** from maternal grandfather to grandson through the mother.

synthetic (adjective)

    not of natural origin

    It is difficult to see the difference between high-quality **synthetic** diamonds and naturally occurring ones.

vital (adjective)

    necessary; important or essential to life

    Availability of water is **vital** to animal and plant life.

meager (adjective)

    deficient; barely sufficient in quantity

    Many areas of the world have periods of drought, when food and water supplies are **meager**.

saline (adjective)

    salty; containing salt

    Saline water can damage or kill plants.

mutant (adjective)

    genetically unexpected; different from its parents

    In humans unpigmented skin, eyes, and hair, known as albinism, is caused by a **mutant** gene.

nutrient (noun)

    food; high-quality feeding substance necessary for life

    Children need a diet high in **nutrients**.

dose (noun)

    one application of a medicine or other treatment modality prescribed by a doctor

    The usual adult **dose** of aspirin for headache is ten grains.

tolerance (noun)

    physical resistance to a noxious agent; acceptance

    Dark-skinned people have a higher **tolerance** for sunlight than fair-skinned people do.

generation (noun)

    offspring of the same parents

    Many genetic traits are passed along from **generation** to **generation**.

strand (noun)

    one string or one fiber

    Cloth is woven from many **strands** of cotton.

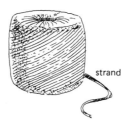

strand

segment (noun)

    any of the clearly differentiated parts an object can naturally be divided into

    Many insects have bodies made up of **segments**.

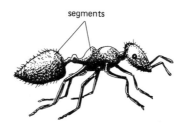

segments

fragment (noun)

    any small, incomplete piece of a whole object, often torn off from the whole

    Sand is made up of **fragments** of rocks.

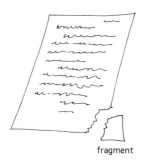

fragment

host (noun)

> organism that houses another organism

> In order to complete their life cycle, parasites must find a **host**.

Vocabulary of Ideas

endeavor (noun)

> effort; attempt; project requiring much work

> Stopping acid rain is a difficult **endeavor,** but an essential one.

to strive (verb)

> to try very hard; to struggle

> Botanists and agronomists **are striving** to make amaranth an economically feasible food crop in the near future.

to undergo (verb)

> to experience; to go through

> This patient **has undergone** three operations to correct his problem.

Vocabulary Exercises

A. Complete the following sentences with words from the list.

nutrients	endeavor	dose
strands	tolerance	generations
segments	fragments	host

1. Finding a cure for cancer is a difficult _____ that many research scientists have devoted their lives to.

2. A diet containing only two or three items is probably deficient in

_____.

3. A large _____ of radiation is often used in cancer therapy.

4. The rope is made with _____ of nylon.

5. Future _____ will no longer find the idea of working with robots strange.

6. Some fish have a greater _____ for acid water than others.

7. Many parasites can only survive in a debilitated _____.

8. An ophthalmologist had to extract several _____ of steel from the worker's eye.

9. A chain is made up of _____ called links.

B. Choose the correct lettered response to complete each numbered statement.

1. FBC boilers _____ combustion efficiency.
   a. skip
   b. boost
   c. splice
   d. derive

2. If salt is _____ to broken skin, pain wll result.
   a. mated
   b. spliced
   c. stimulated
   d. applied

3. It is usually impossible to get animals of different species to _____.
   a. boost
   b. stimulate
   c. mate
   d. retain

4. Blue eyes and blond hair are recessive traits and can only be _____ if both parents carry a gene for them.
   a. derived
   b. passed along
   c. applied
   d. boosted

5. Chile is a(n) _____ country; it has mountains to the east, an ocean to the west, a desert to the north, and Antarctica to the south.
   a. passed along
   b. synthetic
   c. saline
   d. isolated

6. Two pieces of movie film can be _____ together.
   a. spliced
   b. isolated
   c. strands
   d. segments

7. Each generation _____ something of the generation that came before it.
   a. boosts
   b. mates
   c. retains
   d. splices

8. A _____ solution is one that contains salt.
   a. synthetic
   b. saline
   c. nutrient
   d. vital

9. Many medicines are _____ from natural substances.
   a. passed along
   b. derived
   c. stimulated
   d. retained

10. A _____ diet, when eaten by a pregnant woman, can be especially harmful to her unborn child.
    a. isolated
    b. skipped
    c. vital
    d. meager

11. The lab technician _____ an important step, ruining the experiment.
    a. passed along
    b. skipped
    c. boosted
    d. applied

12. We are _____ to eliminate the acid rain problem.
    a. striving
    b. boosting
    c. mating
    d. splicing

13. Caffeine _____ the autonomic nervous system and increases heart rate and metabolism.
    a. stimulates
    b. skips
    c. splices
    d. derives

14. Pulse is one of the _____ signs of life.
    a. vital
    b. saline
    c. meager
    d. synthetic

15. _____ sweeteners such as saccharin have been implicated as carcinogens.
    a. Vital
    b. Saline
    c. Synthetic
    d. Nutrient

16. It is impossible to predict the occurrence of a _____ gene.
    a. mutant
    b. fragment
    c. stimulated
    d. synthetic

17. The space shuttle _____ considerable land-based testing before it was launched the first time.
    a. retained
    b. underwent
    c. skipped
    d. boosted

Studying barley roots undergoing genetic engineering experiments

USDA Photo

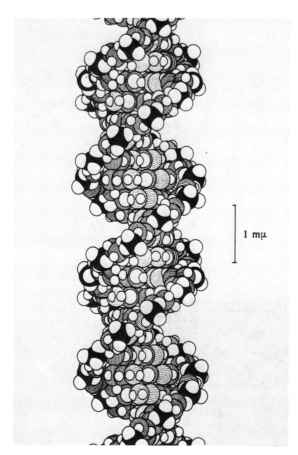

1 mμ

The double helix that composes
the molecular structure of DNA
WHO Photo

Reading Selection

Growing Crops for the Future Through Bioengineering

There was major improvement of hybrid corn, rice, and wheat during a period called the "Green Revolution," which took place during the '60s and the '70s. This agricultural era, in which stress was given to cross-fertilization of plants with the same desirable traits, was a time of crop yield **boosting**. However, growing these cereal crops depended on highly intensified fertilizer programs, many of which were supplied with fertilizers **synthetically** manufactured from petrochemicals. As oil prices soared, no one could guess whether farmers would be able to continue to raise these **vital** crops economically. As a result, agricultural output, which had been on the rise, declined.

New is a second green revolution of another sort. These days, plant geneticists are ascertaining how to develop and breed a broad new array of crops that would have genetic traits allowing them to grow with little or no fertilizer and in areas having **meager** rainfall and **saline** soils. These imaginative scientists are not using conventional breeding methods, such as cross fertilizing plants with desirable traits and then selecting the best ones for creating future offspring. Instead, the process entails **skipping** the sexual **mating** phase and directly transferring the genes themselves from one species to another. This is a challenging **endeavor**, as evidenced by the fact that most plants of different species cannot fertilize each other. Until recently, if farmers wanted an improved variety of corn, they had to use existing genetic traits in corn only. Recent also is the development (described immediately below) of a new breeding technology based on desirable trait combination in new hybrid development. This technology allows geneticists to combine traits of different plants or species.

2

One of these relatively new hybrid breeding methods is tissue culture, in which cells are taken from a plant and then grown *in vitro* in a **nutrient** solution. In one research project, plant geneticists **are striving** to develop crops (such as oats) that can grow and reproduce in saline soils, which are a major problem for many farmers. Their tests involve the use of petri dishes, each of which contains as many as 50,000 cells. The geneticist **applies** large **doses** of salt to each culture, the result of which is that many (but not all) cells die. There may, however, be a few surviving cells, probably having a **mutant** gene for salt **tolerance**. These particular cells **are isolated** and, over a period of time, geneticists will add certain chemicals which **stimulate** the mutuant cells to regenerate into a whole plant. The plant will then be tested over several **generations** in the laboratory to find out if it **retains** the mutant trait and **passes** it **along** to its offspring.

3

in vitro: in glass (in the laboratory)

Another important genetic technique is gene **splicing**, or gene cloning. This technique, referred to as recombinant DNA technology, allows the transfer of genetic material from a plant cell of one species to that of another. DNA, which is a **double-stranded** helix of nucleotide bases with a sugar phosphate backbone, is the genetic material making up most organisms. The gene is a unit that is a **segment** of a DNA molecule and is responsible for controlling hereditary traits, among which are eye and hair coloring.

4

helix: coil or spiral

nucleotide: kind of organic compound

enzymes: proteins produced by a living organism which facilitate biochemical processes within the organism

The first step in gene splicing is for enzymes to be used in cutting out the DNA **fragment** containing the desired genes from a DNA molecule. The enzymes that are used as "scissors" to cut the DNA are called restriction endonucleases. The next step is to cut the DNA from some other organism, such as a bacteriophage or plasmid. Following the bacteriophage or plasmid DNA extraction operation, the two different DNA fragments are joined together by another enzyme, known as a DNA ligase. The new DNA is

5

bacteriophage: microscopic organism that destroys bacteria

plasmid: ring-shaped structure within bacteria

"recombined", from which the term *recombinant DNA* **is derived**. The last step includes a DNA-to-**host**-cell transplant into a host cell that reproduces asexually, but now with a new set of instructions. One use of recombinant DNA technology is to inject the new genes into plant cells for crop nutritive value improvement.

entrepreneurs: investors in business and industry

Tissue culture and recombinant DNA technology are still largely in their infancy and will have **to undergo** more careful testing before we can appreciate the impact they will have. At present, however, many entrepreneurs are ensuring that these new processes will be one of the highest technology industries of the future. One major focus of this industry will be breeding new 6 varieties of vital crops that are drought, blight, and insect-pest resistant and that can grow with little fertilizer. Soon we will know when to expect widespread application of these new technologies. There is no question that many agronomists can expect to have planted the improved hybrids before much time has passed.

Comprehension

EXERCISE

C. Mark the following statements T if they are true or F if they are false.

_____ 1. The "Green Revolution" was a political movement of the '60s and the '70s.

_____ 2. There was great interest in improving cereal crop yields during the "Green Revolution."

_____ 3. Three improved hybrids of that period were corn, rice, and wheat.

_____ 4. Farmers crossed plants with the same desirable traits to produce improved hybrids during the "Green Revolution."

_____ 5. One problem that arose during that period was an increase in the cost of fertilizers.

_____ 6. Only natural fertilizers were used during the "Green Revolution."

_____ 7. Crop yields never went on the decline once the "Green Revolution" began.

_____ 8. A new green revolution has started.

_____ 9. Plant geneticists are striving to develop crops that are less fertilizer dependent.

_____ 10. Cross-fertilizing plants with desirable traits is a major feature of the new green revolution.

_____ 11. The new green revolution emphasizes the sexual mating phase.

_____ 12. Transferring the genetic material directly from one species to another is not difficult.

_____ 13. It is easy to cross different species.

_____ 14. Tissue culture is not a recent phenomenon.

_____ 15. In tissue culture, cells are grown in the laboratory.

_____ 16. Saline soils generally inhibit plant growth.

_____ 17. Petri dishes are used to culture the plant cells.

_____ 18. Salt is used to promote the growth of the plant cells.

_____ 19. The salt causes many of the cells to die.

_____ 20. Those that survive are unusually resistant to a saline environment.

_____ 21. The resistant cells are separated from the others.

_____ 22. These cells then regenerate without the assistance of geneticists.

_____ 23. As soon as the cells become a whole plant, the experiment is finished.

_____ 24. It is important to look at more than one generation of offspring to see the effect of the tissue culture technique of genetic engineering.

_____ 25. In gene splicing, genetic material is transferred directly _in vitro_ from one species to another.

_____ 26. The genetic material making up most organisms is DNA.

_____ 27. Genes are made up of pieces of DNA.

_____ 28. Genes control eye and hair coloring.

_____ 29. In recombinant DNA technology, restriction endonucleases are used for cutting the fragment from the DNA molecule.

_____ 30. A very small real pair of scissors is used.

_____ 31. Next, a fragment of DNA is taken from a bacteriophage or a plasmid.

_____ 32. The two fragments are then spliced by means of a DNA ligase.

_____ 33. Following the joining of the first fragment to the second fragment, the whole unit is transplanted into a host cell.

_____ 34. The transplant should alter the expected offspring of the host cell.

_____ 35. No application of this new technology is yet imagined.

_____ 36. These genetic engineering technologies are already in worldwide use.

Vocabulary in Context

EXERCISE

D. Choose the correct lettered response to define each numbered word or phrase.

1. era (¶ 1)
   a. period of time
   b. equality for women

2. stress (¶ 1)
   a. pressure buildup
   b. emphasis

3. intensified (¶ 1)
   a. concentrated
   b. nervous

4. petrochemicals (¶ 1)
   a. synthetic chemicals
   b. chemicals derived from oil

5. soared (¶ 1)
   a. increased
   b. decreased

6. broad (¶ 2)
   a. wide
   b. bred

7. phase (¶ 2)
   a. step
   b. enzyme

8. culture (¶ 3)
   a. induced growth
   b. art

9. petri dishes (¶ 3)
   a. dishes of oil
   b. dishes for cultures

10. making up (¶ 4)
    a. constituting
    b. destroying

11. hereditary (¶ 4)
    a. which can be passed along genetically
    b. mutant

12. asexually (¶ 5)
    a. nonsexually
    b. only one sex

13. resistant (¶ 6)
    a. tolerant
    b. intolerant

Drawing Conclusions

EXERCISE

E. Choose a or b to answer each question.

1. Why did Green Revolution-era agronomists want to cross plants with the same desirable traits?
   a. in order to create better hybrids
   b. in order to decrease dependence on synthetically manufactured fertilizers

2. How did the fact that most fertilizers were manufactured from petrochemicals cause crop yields to decline?
   a. Farmers couldn't afford to use sufficient amounts of fertilizer to maintain agricultural output.
   b. Most plants have no tolerance for an oily environment.

A scientist studies genetic material within the cell projected on the screen.

Hank Morgan, Photo Researchers, Inc.

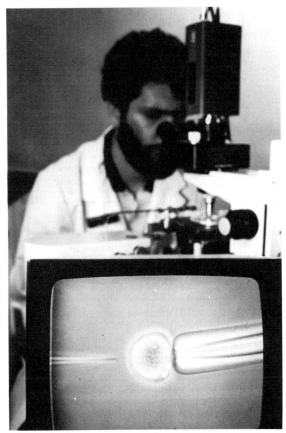

3. How does the new Green Revolution differ from the old one?
   a. The first Green Revolution improved existing plants through hybridization, while the second Green Revolution improves the species by using genetic engineering to combine very dissimilar species at the genetic level.
   b. The old Green Revolution improved crop yields, while the new Green Revolution is interested only in fertilizer dependence.

4. Why is it important to watch the "engineered" plant over several generations?
   a. because the mutant trait is desirable and represents an improvement.
   b. because the trait could be dangerous to the species as a whole

COMPREHENSION SKILL INDEX　　　　　　　　　　　Adjective Clauses

In Lesson 5 attention was given to adjective clauses of the following type:

examples:　　This is the course *in which I developed an interest in genetic engineering.*

　　　　　　It is impossible to predict the factors *against which this treatment modality will have to struggle.*

In addition to this type of adjective clause, another variety exists. This type often uses expressions of quantity. As in all such constructions, the problems in comprehension are probably caused by the word order in the adjective clause and/or the position of insertion within the main clause.

examples:　　These plants, *only a few of which are resistant to a saline environment,* are now available for planting. (Instead of: These plants are now available for planting. Only a few of the plants are resistant to a saline environment.)

　　　　　　She taught several courses last semester, *none of which included a laboratory section.* (Instead of: She taught several courses last semester. None of the courses included a laboratory section.)

Adjective Clauses

EXERCISE

F. Demonstrate your understanding of all types of adjective clauses. Choose the lettered response closer in meaning to the italicized element in each of the following sentences taken from the reading on pages 158-160.

1. This agricultural era, *in which stress was given to cross-fertilization of plants with the same desirable traits*, was a time of crop yield boosting.
   a. when stress was given to cross-fertilization of plants with the same desirable traits,
   b. in stress, which was given to cross-fertilization of plants with the same desirable traits,

2. However, growing these cereal crops depended on highly intensified fertilizer programs, *many of which were supplied with fertilizers synthetically manufactured from petrochemicals.*
   a. which were largely supplied with fertilizers synthetically manufactured from petrochemicals
   b. many which supplied fertilizers synthetically manufactured from petrochemicals

3. One of these relatively new hybrid breeding methods is tissue culture, *in which cells are taken from a plant and then grown* in vitro *in a nutrient solution.*
   a. which in cells are taken from a plant and then grown *in vitro* in a nutrient solution
   b. a process where cells are taken from a plant and then grown *in vitro* in a nutrient solution

4. Their tests involve the use of petri dishes, *each of which contains as many as 50,000 cells.*
   a. containing as many as 50,000 cells do
   b. each containing as many as 50,000 cells

5. The gene is a unit that is a segment of a DNA molecule and is responsible for controlling hereditary traits, *among which are eye and hair coloring.*
   a. which are among eye and hair coloring
   b. such as eye and hair coloring

COMPREHENSION SKILL INDEX

Adjective Clauses: Restrictive vs. Nonrestrictive (Review)

Review the distinction between restrictive and nonrestrictive adjective clauses.

examples:

Restrictive

The boilers *which are in use in most residential buildings* use conventional combustion technology. (The clause describes only that group of boilers in most residential buildings, although other boilers in addition to these do exist.)

The dog *that bit the child* had to be isolated for a period of time. (The clause describes only one particular dog: the one that bit the child, although there are other dogs in addition to this one.)

Nonrestrictive

FBC boilers, *which are not yet manufactured for residential use,* may be widely available in the future. (The clause refers to FBC boilers in general, and there are no other FBC boilers besides those mentioned in the sentence.)

The dog, *which is referred to as "man's best friend,"* can occasionally be unfriendly. (The clause refers to all dogs.)

Remember: One clue is the use of the comma. Restrictive clauses do not use a comma, while nonrestrictive clauses do.

Adjective Clauses:
Restrictive vs. Nonrestrictive (Review)

EXERCISE

G. Circle the antecedent to each of the following italicized clauses in statements adapted from the reading on pages 158-160. Then choose the correct lettered response to indicate your understanding of restrictive and nonrestrictive clauses.

1. There was major genetic improvement of hybrid corn, rice, and wheat during a period called the "Green Revolution," *which took place during the '60s and '70s.*
   a. implies the existence of only one green revolution
   b. implies the existence of more than one green revolution

2. As a result, agricultural output, *which had been on the rise,* declined.
   a. describes just the agricultural output which had been on the rise
   b. describes agricultural output in general

3. These days, plant geneticists are ascertaining how to develop and breed a broad new array of crops *that would have genetic traits allowing them to grow with little or no fertilizer and in areas having meager rainfall and saline soils.*
   a. describes only one group of crops
   b. describes crops in general

4. In one research project plant geneticists are striving to develop crops (such as oats) *that can grow and reproduce in saline soils,* which are a major problem for many farmers.
   a. describes only one special group of crops
   b. describes crops in general

5. In one research project plant geneticists are striving to develop crops (such as oats) that can grow and reproduce in saline soils, *which are a major problem for many farmers.*
   a. describes only those saline soils that are a major problem for many farmers
   b. describes saline soils in general

6. DNA, *which is a double-stranded helix of nucleotide bases with a sugar phosphate backbone,* is the genetic material making up most organisms.
   a. describes one class of DNA
   b. describes DNA in general

7. The enzymes *that are used as "scissors" to cut the DNA* are called restriction endo-nucleases.
   a. describes some specific enzymes
   b. describes all enzymes

8. One major focus of this industry will be breeding new varieties of vital crops *that are drought, blight, and insect-pest resistant and that can grow with little fertilizer.*
   a. describes one specific type of crop
   b. describes all vital crops

Reduced Adjective Clauses (Review)

EXERCISE

H. Each of the following reduced adjective clauses is taken from the reading on pages 158-160. Find each clause in the reading and write down the antecedent it describes.

1. called the "Green Revolution." _____

2. allowing them to grow with little or no fertilizer _____

3. having meager rainfall and saline soils _____

4. including cross-fertilizing plants with desirable traits _____

5. based on desirable trait combination _____

6. probably having a mutant gene for salt tolerance _____

7. referred to as recombinant DNA technology _____

8. making up most organisms _____

9. containing the desired genes from a DNA molecule _____

10. known as a DNA ligase _____

Vocabulary Review

EXERCISE

I. For each of the following words or expressions, find the review vocabulary word in the reading that has the same meaning.

1. permitting _____

2. involves _____

3. product of sexual reproduction _____

4. disease or life-threatening condition of plants _____

5. parasitic organism _____

6. understand _____

7. variety _____

8. output, production _____

9. harvestable plant _____

10. characteristics _____

11. decreased _____

12. learning _____

13. kind or variety of living organism _____

14. group of attached cells _____

15. entail _____

16. remaining alive _____

17. effect _____

18. place of great interest _____

19. mostly _____

20. as proven by _____

21. difficult _____

22. traditional, ordinary _____

23. create _____

24. needed _____

25. insert through use of a needle _____

26. variety _____

27. production _____

From Piston to Propfan: Evolution of the Aircraft Engine

Allison T56–A-15 with turboprop engines

Subtechnical Vocabulary

to opt for (phrasal verb)

to choose; to make a decision

Given a choice between air and rail travel, most travelers **would** probably **opt for** all air travel.

to obtain (verb)

to get; to receive

She **obtained** her doctorate after three years of graduate study.

to ram (verb)

to push violently and hard; to push something into place

The train's brakes failed, and it **rammed** into another train stopped in front of it.

to discharge (verb)

to release; to emit

Factories must find safe ways **to discharge** byproducts of the manufacturing process.

share (noun)

portion; part

Industry is responsible for a large **share** of the acid rain problem.

turbine (noun)

an energy-generating machine that produces power by moving fluid around a wheel or cylinder

Many **turbine** engines use gasoline to provide power.

haul (noun)

distance over which something travels

Electric cars are not as suitable for long **hauls** as gasoline-powered cars.

piston (noun)

solid cylinder which fits inside a hollow cylinder and which moves up and down in response to changing pressure

Pistons are used in all gasoline-powered automobiles.

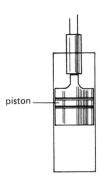

compressor (noun)

machine used to exert pressure on gases

A **compressor** forms part of some household appliances, such as the refrigerator.

chamber (noun)

enclosed space or compartment forming part of a larger object

The combustion **chamber** is the largest part of a furnace or boiler.

thrust (noun)

power of forward movement, particularly in a jet or rocket, caused by the forceful rearward emission of exhaust gases

In a rocket, **thrust** is periodically increased several times during takeoff by the ignition of a new stage.

casing (noun)

container or outer cover

Casings are used to protect delicate machinery.

fan (noun)

machine that moves air by means of a set of blades that rotate around a central core

A **fan** can be used for cooling an area or for facilitating the emission of smoke from a combustion chamber.

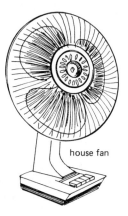

house fan

gear (noun)

round, toothed machine part that fits into another one to change directions or speed, or to transfer movement

Most cars have four forward **gears** as well as reverse.

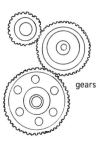

gears

exhaust (noun)

gases released by an engine

Automobile **exhaust** is a major source of air pollution.

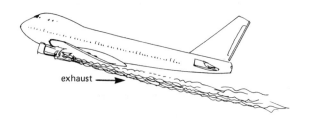

exhaust ➝

laminate (noun)

> manufactured product consisting of bonded layers
>
> Plywood, used instead of solid wood, is a **laminate**.

reliability (noun)

> dependability; trustworthiness
>
> **Reliability** is an essential characteristic of a good airplane.

stiff (adjective)

> rigid; difficult to bend; inflexible
>
> Wood is **stiff**; rubber is flexible.

Vocabulary of Ideas

underway

> in progress; started; in operation
>
> Research on shark blood is **underway**.

on the drawing board

> in the planning stage; not yet underway
>
> Several earthquake prediction systems are **on the drawing board**.

prime (adjective)

> major; best; excellent
>
> The 1906 San Francisco earthquake is a **prime** example of how much damage an earthquake can cause.

Vocabulary Exercises

A. Complete the following sentences with words from the list.

thrust	piston	compressor	gear
fan	exhaust	turbine	laminate
rammed	chamber	haul	casing

1. In hot weather a _____ can help keep you comfortable by circulating the air.

2. Rocket engines generate more _____ than simple jet engines do.

3. A _____ is needed to exert pressure on air inside an engine.

4. An engine which has a design based on a circular configuration is a

_____.

5. A _____ is an engine part that is not stationary when the engine is running.

6. The _____ emissions of gasoline-powered vehicles should be reduced.

7. This machine has a _____ that serves as a permanent protective cover.

8. This table is not made of solid wood; it is made of a plastic

_____.

A turboprop undergoing testing in a propfan program
NASA

NASA 83-HC-534

Conventional jet aircraft
U.S. Air Force Photo

9. A _____ must be replaced if any of its teeth are broken.

10. During aerodynamic testing, a car is placed inside the _____ of a wind tunnel.

11. Propeller-driven aircraft are short-_____ aircraft.

B. Choose the word or expression that best completes each statement.

1. His (exhaust/share) of the work is to operate the controls.

2. Air is compressed by being (rammed/obtained) into a compressor.

3. Sulfur emissions (obtained/discharged) into the air are a health hazard.

4. We are unable to predict earthquakes with a high degree of (thrust/reliability).

5. Of (prime/stiff) importance in the choice of a jet engine is its thrust potential.

6. Certain drugs can be (opted for/obtained) only with a doctor's prescription.

7. Plans for introducing amaranth as a major food crop are still (underway/on the drawing board).

8. A plant that is not (stiff/underway) needs frequent watering.

9. Choosing something is (ramming/opting for) it.

10. Plans for conversion to FBC boilers are (obtained/underway) in many industrial institutions.

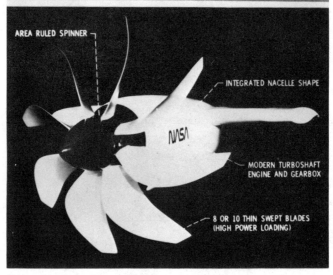

ADVANCED TURBOPROP PROPULSION SYSTEM

AREA RULED SPINNER

INTEGRATED NACELLE SHAPE

NASA

MODERN TURBOSHAFT
ENGINE AND GEARBOX

8 OR 10 THIN SWEPT BLADES
(HIGH POWER LOADING)

Diagram of an advanced turboprop aircraft engine
NASA

Reading Selection

From Piston to Propfan: Evolution of the Aircraft Engine

pinwheel: child's toy
that turns when air is
blown on it

Aerospace engineering development of a radical new kind of aircraft engine known as a propfan is currently **underway**. This turbojet-driven engine contains a large, unconventional-looking, pinwheel-shaped external propeller. Experts believe that the propfan would provide a 25- to 30-percent increase in fuel efficiency over that of present aircraft engines. With fuel economy like that, many airlines **will** certainly **opt for** the development of the propfan, since fuel costs account for a greater than 50-percent **share** of their current operating costs.   **1**

Turbine-powered engines are presently employed in virtually all commercial, private, cargo, and corporate planes used for medium and long **hauls**. The only **piston**-driven aircraft are those that have a less than 300- to 400-horsepower requirement. The **prime** advantage of the turbine over the piston-driven engine is the less expensive fuel   **2**

operating capacity of the turbine engine in most aircraft. To that are added its greater **reliability** and longer life.

The gas turbine engine consists essentially of a three main stage construction. These are an air **compressor,** a combustion **chamber,** and a turbine consisting of a series of **fans.** Air **is rammed** into the compressor, where it is compressed. As the air pressure increases, the air volume decreases until maximum compression is reached. Then this extremely hot air flows through tubes leading to **3** the combustion chamber, where it is mixed with fuel. The resulting hot gases rush out the rear through the turbine, this consisting of rotating blades, which, in turn, drive the compressor. In this way, the jet engine sets up a reaction that continues as long as fuel is provided.

Probably the earliest commercial gas turbine engine was the turboprop, which was developed in the late 1950s. This engine actually consisted of a jet engine and a set of reduction **gears** through which a turbine turned a propeller to produce **thrust.** Additional thrust was also provided from the jet **exhaust.** The turboprop could power a plane at up to 720-kilometer-per-hour speeds, which were faster than those of piston-driven aircraft. During this period, however, the larger commercial airlines decided to use pure jet engines (turbojets) on their aircraft. The turbojet used more **4** fuel than the turboprop, but the jet could propel a plane higher, faster, and more smoothly. Unlike the turboprop, this engine **obtained** all its thrust from hot gases **discharged** rearward through the exhaust nozzle. In this more advanced engine, engineers measure the propulsive ability of the engine in kilograms of thrust instead of horsepower. Today's turbojet engines range in size from small units that supply a few hundred kilograms of thrust to ones that supply thousands of kilograms of thrust.

In the 1960s the first turbofan jets went into service on most aircraft. The turbofan combines the features of the turbojet with those of the turboprop. The turbofan consists of a compressor/ combustor turbine and a power turbine that drives a low-pressure-ratio compressor called a fan. The fan acts like the propeller, as it blows air over and around the engine as well as through it. This gives more thrust and contributes to the aerodynamics of the plane. **5** Unlike the external propeller, the fan is housed inside an outer **casing** called a nacelle, and it is unnoticeable. The engine provides thrust by pushing up to five times as much air through the fan as through the engine core. The fan provides a 30- to 75-percent share of the thrust most commercial jets deliver today. Like a pure jet engine, this engine can drive an airliner at near sonic speeds, while retaining some of the turboprop's fuel efficiency.

concur: agree

Designers in many countries now concur that an external fan or propeller can generate more thrust per engine revolution and in doing so use less fuel than the turbofans. Their idea is to develop a propfan consisting of a large external propeller attached to a turbine. The design of the propeller would not consist of a standard three or four blades, but instead would have between eight and twelve short blades, each shaped like a scimitar to reduce drag caused by supersonic airflow, in much the way a swept wing does. The blades would be made of a special carbon fiber **laminate** which is **stiffer** and lighter than metal. The propfan would produce almost all of its total thrust from its propeller (although the heated exhaust of the turbine would continue to supply a little thrust). If this idea, which is still **on the drawing board**, can be realized, the propfans will certainly be more cost effective than the turbofans. However, more engine innovations will have to be developed and more wind tunnel trials must be conducted before the propfan is ready to fly.

6

scimitar: sword with curved blades

Many aerospace experts believe that this kind of engine will be ready in a few short years. The first commercial airliners to use such engines will probably be the intermediate-sized planes designed for short (2000 kilometers or less) flights.

7

Comprehension

EXERCISE

C. Mark the following statements T if they are true or F if they are false.

_____ 1. A propfan is an old aircraft engine.

_____ 2. The pinwheel-shaped propeller is on the inside of the turbojet-driven engine.

_____ 3. The propfan is relatively fuel efficient.

_____ 4. A large share of the airlines' operating costs is for fuel.

_____ 5. The airlines will probably have only a marginal interest in propfan development.

_____ 6. Most nonmilitary aircraft are powered by turbine- rather than piston-driven engines.

_____ 7. The piston-driven engine is more fuel-efficient than the turbine.

_____ 8. Piston-driven engines are more reliable than turbines.

_____ 9. The three parts of a turbine engine are the compressor, a combustion chamber, and a turbine.

_____ 10. Air volume increases as air is compressed.

_____ 11. In the combustion chamber fuel is combined with heated air.

_____ 12. The reaction is self-sustaining as long as there is enough fuel.

_____ 13. The turboprop was probably the first gas turbine engine used in commercial aircraft.

_____ 14. This engine did not include a propeller.

_____ 15. Thrust resulted from the activity of the propeller and the jet exhaust.

_____ 16. The turboprop made planes go faster than piston-driven engines could.

_____ 17. Pure jets are referred to as turbojets.

_____ 18. The turboprops are faster, can go higher, and ride more smoothly than the turbojets.

_____ 19. The difference between the turboprop and the turbojet is that the turboprop gets all its thrust from the propeller.

_____ 20. The exhaust nozzle propels the hot gases in the direction of the front of the plane.

_____ 21. All turbojets deliver the same amount of thrust.

_____ 22. The turbofan rides outside the engine.

_____ 23. The propfan is an internal fan.

_____ 24. Most of the thrust generated by the propfan would come from the propeller.

_____ 25. Manufacture of the propfan is already underway.

Vocabulary in Context

EXERCISE

D. Choose the correct lettered response to define each numbered word.

1. power (¶ 4)
   a. drive
   b. force

2. pure (¶ 4)
   a. entirely
   b. unspoiled

3. nozzle (¶ 4)
   a. entrance
   b. opening

4. housed (¶ 5)
   a. placed
   b. built

5. realized (¶ 6)
   a. accomplished
   b. noticed

Reference

In order to avoid using the same noun or noun plus modifiers over and over again, writers use general words and phrases that substitute for them. Some examples of these words and phrases are: *this, that, these, those, it, its,* and so on.

The more complex a piece of writing is, the more often these words and expressions are used. The following exercise will begin to make you aware of how often a word or phrase refers to or substitutes for another, and will give you practice in identifying what these words and expressions refer to.

The supersonic aircraft Concorde

Courtesy Air France

Reference

EXERCISE

E. Indicate your understanding of the italicized element in each of the following sentences taken from the reading on pages 176-178 by choosing the correct lettered response. In some cases you will need to look back at the reading to find the answer.

1. Experts believe that the propfan would provide a 25- to 30-percent increase in fuel efficiency over *that* of present aircraft engines.
   a. increase
   b. fuel efficiency

2. With fuel economy like *that*, many airlines will certainly opt for the development of the propfan, since fuel costs account for a greater than 50-percent share of their current operating costs.
   a. development of the propfan
   b. fuel economy

3. With fuel economy like that, many airlines will certainly opt for the development of the propfan, since fuel costs account for a greater than 50-percent share of *their* current operating costs.
   a. the airlines'
   b. the fuel costs

4. To *that* are added its greater reliability and longer life.
   a. less expensive fuel operating capacity
   b. greater reliability and longer life

5. To that are added *its* greater reliability and longer life.
   a. the turbine's
   b. the piston-driven engine's

6. *These* are an air compressor, a combustion chamber, and a turbine consisting of a series of fans.
   a. the gas turbine engine
   b. the three parts

7. Air is rammed into the compressor, where *it* is compressed.
   a. air
   b. the compressor

8. Then this extremely hot air flows through tubes leading to the combustion chamber, where *it* is mixed with fuel.
   a. hot air
   b. the combustion chamber

9. The turboprop could power a plane at up to 720-kilometer-per-hour speeds, which were faster than *those* of piston-driven aircraft.
   a. speeds
   b. kilometers

10. During *this* period, however, the larger commercial airlines decided to use pure jet engines (turbojets) on their aircraft.
    a. the up-to-720-kilometer-per-hour speeds
    b. the late 1950s

11. Unlike the turboprop, this engine obtained all *its* thrust from hot gases discharged rearward through the exhaust nozzle.
    a. the turbojet engine's
    b. the turboprop engine's

12. In *this* more advanced engine, engineers measure the propulsive ability of the engine in kilograms of thrust instead of horsepower.
    a. the turbojet engine's
    b. the turboprop engine's

13. The turbofan combines the features of the turbojet with *those* of the turboprop.
    a. features
    b. the turbofans

14. The fan acts like the propeller, as it blows air over and around the engine as well as through *it*.
    a. the engine
    b. the air

15. Unlike the external propeller, the fan is housed inside an outer casing called a nacelle, and *it* is unnoticeable.
    a. the nacelle
    b. the fan

16. Designers in many countries now concur that an external fan or propeller can generate more thrust per engine revolution and in *doing so* use less fuel than the turbofans.
    a. generating thrust
    b. concurring

17. *Their* idea is to develop a propfan consisting of a larger external propeller attached to a turbine.
    a. countries
    b. designers

18. The design of the propeller would not consist of a standard three or four blades, but instead would have between eight and twelve short blades, *each* shaped like a scimitar to reduce drag caused by supersonic airflow, in much the way a swept wing does.
    a. propellers
    b. blades

19. The design of the propeller would not consist of a standard three or four blades, but instead would have between eight and twelve short blades, each shaped like a scimitar to reduce drag caused by supersonic airflow, in much the way a swept wing *does*.
    a. reduces drag
    b. has between eight and twelve short blades

20. If *this* idea, which is still on the drawing board, can be realized, the propfans will certainly be more cost effective than the turbofans.
    a. to use propfans
    b. to supply thrust
21. The first commercial airliners to use *such* engines will probably be the intermediate-sized planes designed for short (2000 kilometers or less) flights.
    a. airliners
    b. propfans

Vocabulary Review

EXERCISE

F. Match each vocabulary review word taken from the reading on pages 176-178 in column a with its synonym in column b.

a	*b*
1. account for	burning
2. current	creates
3. employed	largely
4. virtually	nonpassenger
5. cargo	present
6. essentially	make up
7. consists of	performed
8. combustion	deliver
9. tubes	drive
10. fuel	decrease
11. sets up	energy provider
12. set	is made up
13. propel	cylindrical passages
14. supply	series of
15. retaining	provide
16. generate	air resistance
17. reduce	almost
18. drag	keeping
19. conducted	used

Vocabulary

BOOK 2

Alphabetical listing of Subtechnical Vocabulary and Vocabulary of Ideas with reference to the lesson the word comes from

abundant	7	(in) between	2	
accessibility	4	(to) blend in	3	
according to	4	(to) block	5	
actually	1	(to) boost	9	
additionally	8	borderline	5	
adjunct	2	buoyancy	6	
anomaly	1	byproduct	8	
apparatus	4	(to) calibrate	5	
appliance	2	camouflage	3	
(to) apply	9	carcinogenesis	1	
(to) appreciate	4	casing	10	
(to) arise	6	(to) cast	2	
array	8	cessation	5	
articulated	2	chamber	10	
(to) ascend	4	chiefly	3	
(to) ascertain	3	chronic	5	
(to) assemble	2	circuit	7	
assembly line	2	(to) coincide	6	
(to) assess	1	coma	4	
(to) assume	6	(to) compensate	5	
bed	8	compressor	10	
(to) behave	1	(to) comprise	3	
(to) belong	3	(to) confirm	3	

malignancy	1		release	8
marked	6		relief	5
mass	6		reliability	10
mass produced	7		remains	3
(to) mate	9		(to) retain	9
materially	7		(to) revert	1
meager	9		rigid	6
mean	4		(to) rule out	6
measure	5		saline	9
mechanism	5		sample	4
modality	5		scarcity	7
mutant	9		sediment	4
naked eye	6		segment	9
noninvasive	1		sensitive	2
norm	5		shadow	7
nutrient	9		share	10
(to) obtain	10		(to) share	3
(to) opt for	10		sheath	1
ore	4		shelter	3
output	5		short-lived	7
(to) outrank	7		side effects	1
(at the) outset	7		significantly	5
overload	5		site	1
paradoxically	1		(to) skip	9
(to) pass along	9		(to) smolder	8
(to) perceive	6		so far	3
phenomenon	6		(to) spare	2
piston	10		(in) spite of the fact	7
(to) postulate	6		(to) splice	9
predominantly	6		spray	2
prevalent	2		stack	2
prime	10		stationary	3
principal	4		stiff	10
(to) probe	1		(to) stimulate	9
(to) program	2		strand	9
progress	1		(to) strive	9
(to) promote	3		subtle	3
propensity	3		superfluous	8
(in) question	1		surroundings	3
quiescence	6		syndrome	4
(to) ram	10		synthetic	9
(to) range	5		(to) take over	2
readout	8		target	1
regardless	5		theoretical	7
(to) regulate	3		thrust	10

Vocabulary

BOOK 1

Alphabetical listing of Subtechnical Vocabulary and Vocabulary of Ideas with reference to the lesson the word comes from

consequently	7	(in) excess of	10
considerable	8	(to) expand	7
(to) consist	6	(to) extend	4
consumption	6	extinct	8
(to) contaminate	8	faced by	9
controls	9	facilities	9
conventional	10	fatality	10
(to) convert	6	feasibility	4
(to) convey	8	feature	7
coronary	2	(to) feed on	5
count	2	ferocious	5
(to) cradle	10	fiber glass	2
crew	9	field	5
crop	4	firstly	7
(to) cross	4	(to) float	10
(to) cultivate	4	force	1
currently	6	(to) forecast	3
(to) cut down on	1	for this reason	7
(on the) cutting edge	10	fossil	8
cycle	5	frequency	5
damage	3	friction	10
(on the) decline	8	fuel	1
decay	3	full-size	1
deck	9	furthermore	8
deep-sea	2	gill	5
delicate	2	(to) generate	6
(to) depend	6	generation	10
deposit	2	(to) glide	9
(to) detach	2	goal	9
(to) develop	3	grain	4
(to) devise	3	ground	3
diameter	6	hardy	4
diet	4	(to) harvest	4
(to) diminish	10	(to) hatch	9
(to) display	9	hazardous	8
(to) distribute	6	hereditary	4
(to) dwindle	6	(to) identify	7
earthquake	3	image	7
ecosystem	8	immediately	10
(to) eject	8	impact	8
(to) emerge	7	(to) indicate	1
(to) emit	2	(to) inhibit	5
(to) encounter	1	(to) initiate	9
environment	4	inner	2
(to) equip	7	(to) insert	2
essential	4	(to) install	1

(to) interact	8	propulsion	10
(to) involve	1	prototype	10
issue	8	quarters	9
(to be) known to	5	(to) race	10
(to) launch	6	ratio	1
(to) lead to	8	reading	3
level	3	(to) record	3
(with) lightning speed	10	(to) reduce	1
like	10	(to be) referred to as	10
maintenance	9	(to) refine	6
maneuvers	9	remedy	8
marginal	4	(to) remove	2
mass	8	(to) renew	6
(to) mature	4	(to) repel	10
(to) miss	4	(to) replace	5
model	1	(to) report	3
moisture	8	resistance	1
(to) monitor	3	resource	6
moreover	8	(as a) result	8
mortality	8	(to) result from	2
moving part	10	retractable	1
network	3	retrieval	9
nevertheless	8	(to) rid	5
noxious	8	row	5
(a) number of	5	scale	3
obstruction	2	(to) scan	7
offspring	4	sequential	7
optical	9	set	5
orbit	6	(to) set up	3
over	3	shade	7
(to) overcome	1	(to) shine	2
(to) overhaul	9	(to be) short of	4
(to) overlap	7	(to) shut off	2
particle	8	signal	7
pattern	7	signs	2
payload	9	(to) simulate	9
personnel	9	slight	3
pest	4	soil	7
(to) pick up	5	some examples	7
pit	5	somewhat	7
plankton	5	(to) sort out	7
potential	7	species	4
(to) precede	3	spectrum	7
(to) pressurize	9	(to) speculate	3
prey	5	(in) spite of	7
(to) propel	9	(to) standardize	7

storage	9	thus	8
streamlined	1	(to) tow	9
stress	3	trait	4
(to) stretch	6	(to) transform	6
stroke	2	tube	2
subject to	1	uniform	4
successive	10	unique	7
(to) suffer from	2	unlike	10
sufficient	6	up to	5
(to) suggest	8	(to) use up	6
(to) supply	2	vacuum	1
surface	3	vibration	10
surgery	2	virtually	10
surveillance	7	waste	6
(to) survive	8	wear and tear	10
suspension	10	(to) wear out	5
(to) sustain	8	wide range of	4
(to) switch on	10	width	1
(to) take a look at	5	wild	4
(to) take (+ time)	4	wing	6
task	9	wire	6
therefore	7	yield	4
(to) threaten	8		

Glossary

The following high-frequency words, in the context used in the text, were chosen for translation as a quick reference device.

ENGLISH	SPANISH	PORTUGUESE
accuracy	exactitud	exatidão
(to) add	añadir	adicionar
(in) advance	por anticipado	antecipadamente
adverse	desfavorable	adverso
aft	a popa	à pôpa; de pôpa
aircraft	aeronave	aeronave
airlock	antecámara de compresión	cãmera de compressão
(to) align	alinearse	alinhar
amount	cantidad	quantidade
angle; at right angles	ángulo; en ángulo recto	ângulo; em ângulo reto
antibody	anticuerpo	anticorpo
around	alrededor de	em volta, em tôrno
(to) arrange	arreglar	arranjar, arrumar
as a whole	generalmente	em conjunto
ash	cenizas	cinzas
(to) assist	ayudar	ajudar
assistant	ayudante	assistente
(to) assume control	tomar control	tomar contrôle
(to) attach	atar	atar, ligar
attachment	unión	ligação, junçao
(to) attend	asistir	assistir
attendant	asistente; ayudante	assistente
available	disponible	aproveitável
average	promedio; término medio	média; médio
(to) avoid	evitar	evitar
aware	consciente	ciente
axis	eje	eixo
back	de atrás	de trás
backache	dolor de espalda	dor nas costas; dor lumbar
back and forth	de atrás para adelante	para trás e para frente
backwards	hacia atrás	para trás
baked	asado al horno	assado, cozido no forno
baking soda	bicarbonato de soda	bicarbonato de sódio
barn	granero	celciro, palheiro
barn owl	lechuza bodeguera	coruja-de-igreja
bay	compartimiento	compartimento
beak	pico	bico
beating	golpeando	batendo
(to) become	llegar a ser	tornar-se, vir a ser
behavior	comportimiento	comportamento
behind	detrás de	atrás, detrás
belief	creencia	crença
(to) believe	creer	crer
bell	campana	campainha
below	abajo; debajo	abaixo, debaixo
belt	cinturón	cinto

ENGLISH	SPANISH	PORTUGUESE
(the) bends	aeroembolia; parálisis de los buzos	mal-dos-caixoēs; mal-dos-mergulhadores
(to) bend	doblar	dobrar
beneath	abajo	abaixo
berry	fruta pequeña como mora, frambuesa, etc.	qualquer fruto do tipo morango, amora, framboesa, etc.
beside	cerca de	ao lado de
beyond	más allá	além
billion	mil millones	bilhão, bilião
bird	pájaro	ave, passaro
birth	nacimiento; parto	nascimento
blade	hoja	fôlha, lâmina
(to) blame	culpar	culpar, responsibilizar
bleeding	flujo de sangre	sangrando
blindness	ceguera	cegueira
blood	sangre	sangue
(to) blow	soplar	soprar
boardlike	como una tabla	como uma tábua
body (of water)	extensión (de agua)	extensão de água
body	cuerpo	corpo
(to) boil	hervir	ferver
boiler	calorífero	caldeira
boldface	negrillas	negrito
bond	grado de afinidad	ligação
bonded	pegado	ligado
bone	hueso	osso
booster	sección propulsadora	foguete reforçador
boring	aburrido	chato, aborrecido
(to be) born	nacer	nascer
bottom	fondo	fundo
box	caja	caixa
brain	cerebro	cérebro
brakes	frenos	freios
(to) break	romper	quebrar, romper
(to) break free	desatarse	libertar-se; desunir-se
(to) breathe	respirar	respirar
bridge	puente	ponte
bright	brillante	brilhante
broad (selection)	amplio	amplo, extenso, largo
broken	quebrado; roto	quebrado; roto
bubble	burbuja	bôlha, borbulha
(to) build	construir; hacer	construir, fazer
building	edificio	edifício
bulb	bombilla	bulbo; lâmpada
burn	quemadura	queimadura
(to) burrow	amadrigarse	fazer toca; escavar
business	comercio; negocio	negócio, comêrcio
cap (polar ice cap)	capa	calota glacial do poío
capable	capaz	capaz
care	cuidado; atención	atenção; cuidado
careful	cuidadoso	cuidadoso
(to) carry	llevar; conducir	carregar, levar
(to) catch	capturar; agarrar	apanhar; agarrar
century	siglo	século
chain	cadena	cadeia
change	cambio	mudança; cámbio
(to) channel	acanalar	acanalar; canalizar
charcoal	carbón de leña	carvão vegetal
checkerboard	tablero (de damas)	tabuleiro (de damas)
chest	pecho	peito
childbirth	parto	parto
chin	mentón	queixo
(to) choose	escoger	escolher

ENGLISH	SPANISH	PORTUGUESE
(to) churn	revolver; agitar	bater; agitar
claw	garra	garra
clean	limpio	limpo
(to) climb	ascender	ascender
close	cerca	perto
cloth	tela	tecido, pano
clothing	ropa	roupa
cloud	nube	nuvem
clue	indicio	indício
coal	carbón de piedra	carvão
(to) coin a word	crear una palabra nueva	inventar uma palavra nova
concern	preocupación	preocupação (interêsse)
conference	consulta	conferência
container	envase; caja	recipiente
conveyance	transporte	transporte
cooking	cocina	arte culinária, cozinha
cooky	galletita	bolacha, biscoito
(to) cool	enfriarse	arrefecer
core	parte central	âmago, centro
corn	maíz	milho, grão
corner	esquina; rincón	esquinha; canto
cost effective	que rinde más beneficio por el coste	a maneira mais eficaz por o custo
costly	caro	custoso
cotton	algodón	algodão
(to) cough	toser	tossir
crack	grieta	greta
cracker	galleta	bolacha
craft	nave; vehículo	nave espacial, nave do espaço
crash	choque	colisão, choque
crawling	andando a cuatro patas	rastejar
(to) cross out	tachar	riscar
cruising speed	velocidad de viaje	velocidade de cruzeiro
crushing	aplastante	esmagante
crust	corteza	crosta
cup	taza	taça
(to) cure	remediar	curar
cure	remedio	cura, remédio
daily	diario	diário
damp	húmedo	úmido
danger	peligro	perigo
dangerous	peligroso	perigoso
dark	oscuro	escuro
(to) date back to	tener su comienzo en	datar de
dead	muerto	morto
(to) deaden	amortiguar	amortecer
(to) deal with	encargarse de	lidar com; ocupar-se com
death	muerte	morte
deathly	cadavérico	mortal
debt	deuda	dívida
(to) decline	disminuir(se)	declinar
(to) decrease	disminuirse	diminuir(-se)
deep	profundo	profundo
degree	grado	grav
(to) deliver	entregar; transmitir	entregar
departure	salida	partida, saída
depressed	hundido; aplanado	deprimido
(to) design	diseñar	designar
(to) destroy	destruir	destruir
(to) detect	percibir; advertir	descobrir
device	aparato	invenção; aparelho
(to) devote	dedicarse	dedicar-se a
dew	rocío	orvalho
dexterity	destreza	destreza

ENGLISH	SPANISH	PORTUGUESE
(to) diffuse	difundir	difundir
dirt	suciedad	sujeira
disagreement	desacuerdo	desacôrdo
(to) discourage	desanimar; disuadir	desencorajar
disease	enfermedad	doença
(to) display	exhibir; mostrar	exibir; mostrar
disturbance	alteración; desarreglo	perturbação; distúrbio
diver	buceador	mergulhar
(to) divide	partir	dividir
diving	buceo	mergulho
dizziness	vértigo	vertigem
donkey	burro	asno
(to) dope	suavizar	aplicar
drag	resistencia al avance	arrastamento; resistência do ar
(to) draw (conclusions)	concluir	concluir
drop	gota	gôta
drought	sequía	sêca
drug	droga	droga
(to) dry	secar	secar
dust	polvo	poeira
ear	oreja	orelha
earth	tierra	terra
earthly	terrestre	terrestre
earth-based	apegado a la tierra	com base na terra
earth-bound	con rumbo a la tierra	com destino a terra
effective	eficaz	eficaz
effort	esfuerzo	esfôrço
empty	vacío	vazio
(to) enact	promulgar	decretar; promulgar
(to) enclose	encerrar; incluir	encerrar
(to) endure	aguantar	suportar, agüentar
(to) engage in	participar (en)	ocupar-se (em); envolver-se (em)
engine	máquina; motor	máquina; motor
enterprise	empresa	emprêsa
entrepreneur	empresario	empreiteiro, empreendador
exposed	expuesto	exposto
extent	grado	grau
fact	hecho	fato
(to) fail	fracasar; dejar de funcionar	falhar; falir
fair-skinned	blanco	tez clara; branco
familiar	conocido	bem conhecido
(to) fasten	fijar; atar	prender; segurar
fats	grasas	gorduras
fault	falla	falta, defeito
feather	pluma	pena, pluma
(to) feed	alimentar; alimentarse (de)	alimentar(-se)
female	hembra	fêmea
fierce	feroz	feroz
fiery	flameante	flamejante, ardente
fight	pelea; lucha	luta
finding	hallazgo	achado; descubrimento
finesse	delicadeza	finura, sutileza
(to) fit	caber; encajar (en)	caber, conformar
(to) fix	reparar	arrumar, consertar
fixed	fijo	fixo
flame	llama	chama
flap	guardafango; alerón	aba, borda
flight	vuelo	vôo
(to) flip	soltar	dar um piparote; saltar
flounder	lenguado	linguado
flour	harina	(flor de) farina
flow	flujo; derrame; corriente	fluxo, corrente
flue	humero; tubo de caldera	fumeiro

ENGLISH	SPANISH	PORTUGUESE
footnote	nota al pie de la página	nota ao pé da página
(to) forecast	pronosticar	prognosticar
forefront	vanguardia	vanguarda
forklift	elevador de carga	empilhadeira de forquilha; carroguindaste
foundry	fundición	fundição
framework	armazón	estrutura/armação
freshwater	(de) agua dulce	(de) agua doce
frightened	asustado	assustado
fuel-efficient	que requiere la menor cantidad de combustible	usar mais combustível
fuel-short	con escasez de combustible	com escassez de
furry	peludo	peludo
fuzzy	indistinto	impreciso
gain	ganancia; aumento	ganho; proveito
galley	cocina	galé
gauge	indicador	calibrador, indicador
(to) grind	moler; rechinar	moer; triturar
(to) grow teeth	echar dientes	endentecer; nascer os dentes
(to) guess	adivinar; suponer	adivinhar
(rain) gutter	canal de lluvia	goteira
(to) hang	colgar; suspender	pendurar; colgar
hardcover	libro encuadernado	livro encadernado
(to) harden	endurecer	endurecer
harm	daño	mal; dano
hawk	halcón	falcão
hay	heno	feno
head lamps	faroles	farois dianteiros
heat	calor	calor
heating	calefacción	aquecimento
hollow	hueco	ôco
hollow	cavidad; depresión	cavidade; vale
hood	cubierta	capuz; capô
hooked	ganchoso	munido de ganchos
(to) hunt	cazar	caçar
(to) hyphenate	escribir con guión	hifenizar
illness	enfermedad	doença
(to) injure	dañar; herir	ferir; injurar
injury	perjuicio; herida	ferimento; injúria
innards	interior; entrañas	tripas, entranhas
insulator	aislador	isolador
(to) interfere	impedir	interferir
investment	inversión	investimento
iron	hierro	ferro
italicized	en letra bastardilla	italicizado; grifado
(to) jettison	tirar	alijar carga (ao mar); tirar fora
joint	articulación	junta; ligação
junk food	comida sin valor nutritivo	comida sem valor nutritívo
keen	agudo	agudo, perspicaz
kidney stone	piedra nefrítica	cálculo renal
(to) kill	matar	matar
(to) label	calificar; apodar	rotular, etiquetar
(to) lace	entretejer	entrelaçar
land-based	con base en tierra	com base na terra
law	ley	lei; direito
layer	estrato	estrato, camada
(to) lead	conducir; dirigir	guiar, conduzir
lead	plomo	chumbo
leaf	hoja	fôlha
lens	lente	lente
lethal	letal; mortal	letal
license plate	placa, tablilla, patente	placa, chapa
lifespan	duración de vida	duração de vida

ENGLISH	SPANISH	PORTUGUESE
liftoff	despegue (de un cohete)	decolagem (de foguete)
light	claro	claro
light	liviano	·eve
light	luz	luz
lightning	relámpago	relâmpago
likely	probable	provável
lime	cal	cal
limestone	caliza	calcário
link	vínculo	elo; argola
log	tronco; leña	tronco; livro de bordo
lonely	solitario; aislado	só; isolado
longstanding	de largos años	duradouro
lung	pulmón	pulmão
machinery	maquinaria	maquinaria
(to) make up for	compensar por	compensar
male	macho	macho
malnutrition	desnutrición	desnutrição
(to) master	conocer a fondo	dominar; tornar-se perito em
(to) match	hacer juego con	igualar; comparar
matter	asunto	assunto
matter	materia	matéria
(to) maximize	aumentar al máximo	maximizar
(to) measure	medir	medir
message	mensaje; comunicación	mensagem
midwife	partera	parteira
mileage	(millaje) kilometraje	milhagem (quilometragem)
(to) minimize	reducir al mínimo; subestimar	reduzir au mínimo
mirror	espejo	espelho
(to) mix	mezclar	misturar
morbidity	morbosidad	morbidez
mud flap	guardafango	páralama
nacelle	barquilla	nacele; barquinha
needle	aguja	agulha
non-prescription	(droga) no recetada	não-receitada
nozzle	boquilla	bico; bocal
nurse	enfermera	enfermeira
oat	avena	aveia
oil shale	esquisto petrolífero	xisto petrolífero
(to be) on the rise	estar subiendo	estar subindo
opening	abertura	abertura
outcome	resultado	resultado
outdoors	(al) aire libre	(ao) ar livre
outer	exterior; externo	exterior; externo
outlook	punto de vista	perspectiva; ponto de vista
(to) outperform	hacer mejor que	ultrapassar; exceder
outpost	puesto fronterizo	pôsto; posição avançado
(to) outweigh	pesar más; importar más que	exceder em pêso; ser mais importante
(to) outwork	trabajar más que	superar no trabalho
overactive	hiperactivo	demasiado ativo
overweight	obeso	obeso
owl	lechuza	coruja
ownership	posesión	propriedade; posse
pain	dolor	dôr
parachute	paracaídas	pára-quedas
passageway	pasadizo	passagem
patch	mancha	remendo; trecho
path	trayectoria	trajetória; trilha
pathway	conducto	caminho
(to) perch	posarse	empoleirar-se; pousar
(to) perform	ejecutar; desempeñar; ejercer	executar
petri dish	cápsula de Petri	o prato em que se faz culturas
phase	fase	fase
physician	médico	médico

ENGLISH	SPANISH	PORTUGUESE
(to) pick	escoger; recoger	escolher
pinwheel	girándula	girândola
pipe	cañaría; tubo	tubo, cano
(to) pipe	encañar	encanar; canalizar
placement	colocación	colocação
plains	llanuras	planicie
plate	plancha	placa
plentiful	abundante	abundante
(to) plug in	enchufar; conectar	fazer ligação; inserir
plywood	madera terciada	madeira compensada
point of view	punto de vista	ponto de vista
pointless	sin sentido	sem sentido
pointed	puntiagudo	pontudo
(to) point out	indicar; señaler	mostrar; chamar atenção para
poison	veneno	veneno
pollution	contaminación	poluição
pond	laguna	pequeno lago
poor	inferior; árido	inferior; infértil
poor	pobre	pobre
poorly	insatisfactoriamente	pobremente
(to) pose (a threat)	amenazar	propor uma ameaga; ameaçar
(to) pour	echar; fluir	fluir, correr
power	poder; energía	poder; energia
practitioner	médico	médico
pregnant	grávida	grávida
(to) prescribe	recetar	receitar
(to) pretend	aparentar	fingir; pretender
procedure	procedimiento	procedimento; processo
prone	propenso	propenso; inclinado
proof	prueba	prova
propeller	hélice	hélice
(to) propel	propulsar	propulsar
(to) provide	proveer	prover
(to) pump	bombear; circular	bombear
puzzle	misterio; problema; rompecabezas	quebra-cabeça; enigma
race horse	caballo corredor	cavalo de corridas
(to) radiate	emitir; irradiar	irradiar; radiar
rail	carril	carril
railroad	ferrocarril	ferrovia
railways	ferrocarril	linhas ferroviárias
rain gutter	canal de lluvia	goteira de chuva
rate	tasa; velocidad; porcentaje	taxa; velocidade; custo
rearward	hacia atrás	de retaguarda; traseiro
recall	memoria	lembrança
(to) recoup	recuperar	reembolsar
(to) redden	enrojecer(se)	avermelhar(-se)
red-hot	calentado al rojo	candente; aquecido ao rubro
reed	junco; caña	junco; cana
(to) refill	rellenar	reabastecer; reencher
(to) rely (on)	depender (de)	contar com
remorse	remordimiento	remorso
research	investigación	pesquisa
(to) retard	atrasar; retardar	atrasar; retardar
(to) return	regresar; volver; devolver	voltar; devolver
reusable	para uso repetido	para uso repetido
ring (of tree)	corte anular	camadas anuaís
risk	riesgo, peligro	risco, perigo
rocket	cohete	foguete
rodent	roedor	roedor
roof	techo	telhado
roost	percha	poleiro, pouso
rope	cuerda	corda
(to) rotate	girar; rotar	girar; rodar

ENGLISH	SPANISH	PORTUGUESE
rough	desigual; quebrado	impolido; irregular
rubber	caucho	borracha
ruff	collarín de plumas	gargantilha, coleira de penas
rules	reglas; leyes	regras; leis
running	funcionando	funcionando
run	prueba	prova
runway	pista	pista de decolagem
sailing	navegación	navegação
(to) save time	ahorrar tiempo	poupar tempo
sawdust	aserrín	serragem, serradura
(to) scatter	esparcir	espalhar
screen	pantalla	écran
scrubber	depurador	esfregador, purificador
scurvy	escurbuto	escorbuto
sea level	nivel del mar	nível do mar
(to) search (for)	buscar; anhelar	procurar, buscar
shallow	poco profundo	raso, pouco profundo
shark	tiburón	tubarão
(to) shift	mudar	mudar; trocar
(to) shorten	acortar; reducir	encurtar
shortness of breath	disnea	falta de fôlego
similar	semejante	semelhante
single	único; individual; singular	único; só; individual
(to) sink	sumergirse; descender	afundar, submergir
skill	habilidad	habilidade
(to) skim	ojear	deslizar à superfície
skull	cráneo	crânio
sleepiness	somnolencia	sonolência
slide rule	regla de cálculo	régua de cálculo
(to) slope	estar en declive	inclinar
(to) slow	retardar; disminuir la velocidad	retardar; diminuir a velocidade
smell	olor; olfato	odor; olfato
smog	humo mezclado con niebla	combinação de nevoeiro e fumaça
smoke	humo	fumaça; fumo
smokestack	chimenea; conducto de humo	chaminé
snout	hocico	focinho
(to) soar	remontarse	voar alto
(to) solve	solucionar	solucionar, resolver
somehow	de algún modo	de algum modo
sore	adolorido	sensível, dolorido
sought after	deseable	desejável, procurado
sound	sonido	som, sonido
source	fuente; origen	fonte; origem
spacecraft	astronave	astronave
speaker	conferenciante; altoparlante	orador, locutor; alto-falante
speed	velocidad	velocidade
speedometer	velocímetro	velocímetro
spelling	ortografía	ortografia
(to) spend time	pasar tiempo	passar tempo
(to) spill	derramar	derramar
spot	sitio	sítio, ponto
spot welding	soldadura de una área muy pequeña	soldadura de precisão
(to) spread	estirarse	estirar; estender
(to) spread out	difundirse	distender; difundir
spring	muelle	mola
square	cuadrado	quadrado
(to) stand for	representar; significar	representar; significar
(to) state	decir; formular	relatar; afirmar
steady	estable; continuo	estável; constante
steam	vapor	vapor
steel	acero	aço
(to) stick together	no separarse	conservar-se unidos
store	depósito; almacen	armázem

ENGLISH	SPANISH	PORTUGUESE
(to) store	almacenar	abastecer; armazenar
(to) straighten out	arreglar(se)	endireitar-se, pôr em ordem
stream	corriente	corrente
string	cuerda	cordão, corda
(to) struggle	luchar	lutar
subject	sujeto	sujeito
success	éxito	êxito
suitable	conveniente	conveniente
sunspot	mácula del sol	mancha solar
(to) superimpose	superponer	sobrepor
(to) support	apoyar; sostener; tolerar	apoiar; sustentar
(to) suppose	suponer	supor
(to) surface	emerger; volver a la superficie	emergir; vir à tona
(to) surmise	conjeturar	imaginar
(to) surpass	superar	superar
(to) surround	rodear; cercar	rodear; cercar
(to) suspect	sospechar	suspeitar
(to) sweep	barrer	varrer
sword	espada	espada
takeoff	despegue	decolagem
(to) take off	quitar(se)	levantar vôo; decolar
(to) take out	sacar; poner afuera	levar para fora, por fora
(to) take place	ocurrir; tener lugar	acontecer; ter lugar
talon	garra	garra
tanker	buque petrolero	(navio) petroleiro
team	equipo	equipe
tenfold	décuplo	décuplo
term	término	têrmo
test tube	tubo de ensayo	tubo de ensaio
threadlike	filiforme	filiforme
throat	garganta	garganta
(to) throw away	botar	deitar fora
tilt	inclinación	inclinação
topmost	predominante	o mais alto
treatment	tratamiento	tratamento
trench	fosa	fôsso
trial	ensayo	ensaio, prova
trim	adorno	alinho; apuro
trouble	inconveniencia	desgraça, dificuldade
underground	subterráneo	subsolo; subterrâneo
undersea	submarino	submarino
underside	parte de abajo	lado inferior
undigested	no digerido	indigerido
unfading	inmarchitable	imarcesível
(to) unscramble	desenrollar	pôr em ordem
unspoiled	no corrumpido	não estragado
vessel	vaso	vaso
warning	advertencia; alarma	aviso
wedge	cuña	cunha
weight	peso	pêso
(to) weld	soldar	soldar
well	pozo	poço
wheat	trigo	trigo
(to) whip	batir; agitar(se)	bater; chicotear
widespread	común; extendido	estendido; muito difundido
windmill	molino de viento	moinho de vento
windshield	parabrisas	párabrisa
wind tunnel	túnel aerodinámico	túnel aerodinâmico
wiring	canalización eléctrica	instalação elétrica; rêde elétrica
worldwide	global	mundial

ENGLISH	JAPANESE	ARABIC
abnormal	異常な	شاذ
absorb	吸収する	يَمتصّ
to accelerate	加速する	يتسارع
accommodations	宿泊設備	وسائل الرّاحة
accumulation	集積	تراكم
accuracy	正確さ	دقة ، صحة
acetylene	アセチレン	الأستيلين
acid	酸	حامض
acrylic	アクリルの	أكريلي ، أكريليك
to activate	作動させる	يُنشّط
adequate	十分な	كافٍ
administration	管理	إدارة
adverse	不利な	مُعاد ، معاكِس
aerodynamic	気体力学	إيرودينامي
aeronautics	航空学	علم الطيران
aerosol	エアゾール	الهباء الجوي ، دُخان
aerospace	大気および宇宙空間の	جو الأرض والفضاء الذي وراءه
agriculture	農業	زراعة
agrology	農業科学	علم التُربة
aircraft	航空機	منطاد أو طائرة
airlock	エアロック	قفل هوائي
air tanks	エアタンク	خزانات هواء
alarming	驚くべき	مُنذر
alkali	アルカリ	قلوي
alternating current	交流	التيار المتردّد أو المتناوب
altitude	高度	الارتفاع
amaranth	アマランス	اللون الأرجواني الداكن
ambiguously	あいまいに	غامض
amino acid	アミノ酸	الحامض الأميني
amoeba	アメーバ	الأميبة
amplification	拡大	تكبير ، تضخيم
anachronism	時代錯誤	المفارقة التاريخية
analysis	分析	تحليل
anatomical	解剖（学上）の	تشريحي
anesthesia	麻酔	فقدان الحس ، الخُدار
antibiotic	抗生物質	مضاد للجراثيم
antibodies	抗体	أجسام مضادة
anti-coagulative	抗凝固性の	مانع التخثُّر
aquiculture	水生生物を養殖すること	تربية الحيوانات والنباتات المائية
aquifer	透水層	طبقة صخرية مائية
architect	建築家	المهندس المعماري
arsenic	ヒ素	زرنيخ
arthritis	関節炎	التهاب المفاصل
artificial	人工の	اصطناعي
asexually	無性の	لا تزاوجي
astronaut	宇宙飛行士	رائد الفضاء
astronomer	天文学者	الفلكي

ENGLISH	JAPANESE	ARABIC
asymptomatic	無症候性の	لا عَرَضي
atherosclerotic	アテローム性動脈硬化症の	منصبّ الشرايين
atmosphere	空気、雰囲気	الغلاف الجوي
atom	原子	الذَّرَّة
to attach	つける	يربط ، يَضُمّ
automatic	自動的な	تلقائي ، أوتوماتيكي
autonomic	自律性の	ذاتي ، مُسْتَقِل
aviation	飛行	الملاحة الجوية
bacteria	バクテリア	جراثيم ، بكتيريا
bacteriophage	バクテリオファージ（ウィルスの一種）	مُلْتَهِم الجراثيم
barometric	気圧の	الباروتري
barometric pressure	気圧上の	الضغط البارومتري
basking shark	ウバザメ	قِرْش مُسْتَدْفِىء ، مُتَشَمِّس
beak	くちばし	منقار
beneficial	有益な	مفيد
biochemistry	生物化学	الكيمياء الحيوية
bioengineering	生物工学	الهندسة الحيوية
biology	生物学	علم الأحياء
biopsy	生体組織検査	استئصال نسيج من الجسد الحي ودراسته مجهرياً
bleeding	出血	نزيف
blindness	盲目	عمى
blood pressure	血圧	ضغط الدم
to boil	沸騰させる	يغلي
boldface	肉太の活字書体の一種	حرف أسود ، الطباعة بحرف أسود
bone	骨	عظم
boron	ホウ素	البورون : عنصر لافلزي يكون في البُوْرَق
botanist	植物学者	عالم النبات
brain	脳	دماغ ، ذكاء
to breathe	呼吸する	يتنفّس
cactus	サボテン	صبّار
caffeine	カフェイン	الكافيين ، البُنِّين
calcium	カルシウム	الكلسيوم
calculation	計算	حساب
calorie	カロリー	سُعْر ، كالوري
cancer	癌	السرطان
capability	能力	قابلية ، قدرة
capacity	収容力	استيعاب
carbohydrate	炭水化物	الكربوهيدرات
carbon dioxide	二酸化炭素	ثاني أكسيد الكربون
carcinoma	癌種	سَرطان ، ورم سرطاني
category	範ちゅう	طبقة ، صِنْف
causation	原因になること	سَبَب
cavity	空洞	فجوة
centrifugal force	遠心力	القوة الطاردة من المركز
characteristic	特性、特徴	مُمَيِّز ، العدد البياني
charge	充電	يَشْحَن
chemotherapy	化学療法	المعالجة (للأمراض) بالمواد الكيمائية
childbirth	出産	الولادة
chlorine	塩素	الكلور
cholesterol	コレステロール	الكولستيرول
chromium	クロム	الكروم
to churn	かき回す	يحرّك بعنف ، يمخض اللبن
to circulate	循環する	يَنْشُر ، يدور
circumference	周囲	محيط الدائرة
circumstance	事情	ظرف ، حاله
to be classified	分類した	أن يكون مُصَنّف
clay	粘土	طين ، وحل
climate	気候	مُنَاخ
cloning	クローン	ارتجاف
clue	手がかり	مفتاح لحل لُغْز
coal	石炭	فحم نباتي
cobalt	コバルト	الكوبالت
coefficient	係数	المسمى (ر) ، المعامل

ENGLISH	JAPANESE	ARABIC
combination	配合	توحيد ، ضمْ
comet	彗星	المُذَنّب
compartment	区画	قسم أو جزء مُسْتَقِلّ ، مقصورة في قطار
complication	複雑	تعقيد
component	構成要素	مركب
to compose	構成する	يُركّب
to concentrate	一点に集中する	يركز ، يكثّف
concentric	同心	متحد المركز
conception	概念	ادراك ، فَهْم ، حمل
concrete	具体物	واقعي ، ملموس
to condense	凝縮する	يُكثّف
cone	円錐形の	مخروط
consequence	結果	نتيجة
conservation	保守	صيانة
constituent	構成している	تأسيسي
construction	建築	إنشاء ، تأسيس
to consume	尽きる	يستنفد ، يستهلك
context	脈絡	سياق الكلام ، بيئة ، محيط
conversion	変換	تحويل
convincing	納得させる	مُقنع
copper	銅	نحاس
core	しん	لُبّ ، جَوْهَر
corporate	団体の	مشترك
correlation	相関関係	علاقة مُتبادلة
cost-effective	費用効果の	إقتصادي
to counteract	反作用する	يُضاد ، يُبطِل
to create	造る	يَخْلق ، يُبدع
cross-fertilization	他家受精	الأخصاب التهجيني
crust	堅くなった表面	الجزء الخارجي من سطح الأرض ، الغلاف
crystal	水晶	بلّور ، شفاف
cure	治癒	علاج
cylinder	シリンダー	الاسطوانة
dam	ダム	سد ، خزّان
data	データ	معلومات ، حقائق ، بيانات
deaden	鈍くする	يميت ، يُخمِد
debilitated	衰弱した	جعله ضعيفاً ، مُضْعَف
decompression	減圧	مزيل للضغط
deficiency	不足	نقص ، عجز
to deform	ゆがめる	يشوه
to demonstrate	明示する	يظهر بوضوح ، يتظاهر
density	密度	كثافة
dentistry	歯科医学	طب الأسنان
dependability	信頼性	إعتمادية
depressed	意気消沈した	مُقعّر السطح الأعلى ، منخفض ، حزين
depths	深さ	أعماق
determination	決定	التصميم ، ثبات في العزم
developing	発展途上にある	متطور ، نامي
device	装置	أداة ، وسيلة
dew	露	ندى
dexterity	機敏さ	براعة
diabetic	糖尿病の	دیابيتي : ذو علاقة بداء البول السكري
to diffuse	拡散する	ينشر (الضوء أو الحرارة)
diluted	薄められた	مُخفّف
dinosaur	恐竜	الدينصور
disaster	災難	كارثة
discouraged	落胆した	مُثبّط الهمّة
disease	病気	مَرض
disintegration	崩壊	انحلال
to dissolve	分解溶解する	يحل ، يُذيب
distortion	ゆがみ	تحريف ، تشويه
disturbance	乱れ	ازعاج ، اقلاق
dizziness	めまい	دوخة ، دوار
doctorate	博士号	درجة (أو لقب) الدكتوراه

ENGLISH	JAPANESE	ARABIC
dolomite	ドロマイト白雲石	الدولوميت
drought	乾燥	جفاف
dryness	乾燥	جفاف
eclipse	（太陽、月などの）食	كسوف (الشمس) ، خسوف (القمر)
ecology	生態学	علم التبيؤ : فرع من علم الاحياء يدرس العلاقات بين الكائنات الحيّة وبيئتها
electrolyte	電解液（質）	الالكتروليت: المنحل بالكهرباء
electromagnet	電磁石	المغنطيس الكهربائي
electron	電子	الالكترون ، الكهيرب : شحنة كهربائية سالبة تشكل جزءاً من الذرة
element	要素	العنصر
to elevate	上げる	يقيم ، يرفع
emission	放出	اطلاق
endocrine	内分泌腺	هرموني
energy	エネルギー	طاقة
engineering	工学	هندسة
enormity	大罪	قباحة ، ضخامة
enterprise	企業	مؤسسة تجارية ، مشروع
entrepreneur	事業者	الملتزم ، المقاول
enzyme	酵素	خميرة ، أنزيمة
equator	赤道	خط الاستواء
ethics	倫理	أخلاق ، علم الأخلاق
etiology	原因	علم أسباب الأمراض
evaporation	蒸発する	تبخر
evolution	進化	تطور ، نشوء
to excrete	排せつする	يُفرز (العرق)
expectancy	予期	توقع
experiment	実験	اختبار ، تجربة
to exploit	開発する	يستخدم ، يستغل
exploration	探査	استكشاف
explosion	爆発	انفجار
eyesight	視力	بَصَر
fair-skinned	白色の肌の	بشرة فاتحة
farmlands	農地	مزرعة أو أرض صالحة للزراعة
fatal	命にかかわる	قدري ، مميت
to fertilize	受精する	يُلقَح ، يُسمَد
fever	熱	حمى
fiber	繊維	نسيج ، خيط أو شيء كالخيط
fierce	ものすごく恐しい顔付きの	قوي ، مفترس
filter	フィルター	مصفاة
firefighter	消防士	رجل إطفاء
flame	炎	لهب
flowing	流れるような	جريان
flue	煙管	مَشرب ، مدخنة
fluid	流動体	سائل
foodstuff	栄養素	مادة غذائية
to forage	食糧をあさる	يهب ، بطوف بحثاً عن العلف أوالطعام
to forecast	予報する	يتنبأ ، يتكهن (بحالة الجو)
to foresee	先見する	يتنبـأ ، يتوقع أو يدرك قبل الحدوث
forklift	フォークリフト	الرافعة المشعبّة : رافعة ذات أصابع فولاذية تُقحم تحت الحمل
formulae	公式（複）	صيغة ، غذاء بديل عن اللبن (لتغذية الطفل)
foundry	鋳込み	مسبوكات ، مسبك المعادن
fragile	弱い	سهل المكسر ، هش
to function	働く	يؤدي (عملاً معيناً)
galaxy	銀河	المجرّة
gaseous	ガス状の	غازي
gene	遺伝子	الجينة ، المورّثة
genetics	遺伝学	علم الوراثة
genus	膝（複）	جنس ، طبقة
geological	地質学の	جيولوجي : خاص أو متعلق بعلم طبقات الأرض
geomorphic	地球の形の	جيومورفي : خاص بشكل الأرض أو سمات سطحها
geothermal	地熱の	حراري أرضي
germ	微生物	ميكروب ، جرثومة

ENGLISH	JAPANESE	ARABIC
gland	腺	غُدّة
glucose	ぶどう糖	الغلوكوز : سكّر العنب ، سكر النشاء
graph	グラフ	شيء مكتوب أو مرسوم
gravity	引力	جاذبية الأرض
grid	方眼	المِصْيَعَة : شبكة قضبان مُتصالبة
to grow	育てる	ينمو ، ينبت
guessing	推量	تخمين ، حَزر
gutters	樋	مزاريب ، قنوات
habit	習性	عادة
habitat	生息地	الموطن : بيئة الحيوان أو النبات
to harden	硬化する	يُقَسّي
harmful	有害な	مُؤذٍ ، ضار
hawk	タカ	صقر
hazard	危険、冒険	مخاطرة
headache	頭痛	صُداع
health	健康	ازدهار ، صحة
heartbeat	心拍	نبضة قلب
hectare	ヘクタール	الهكتار : عشرة آلاف مترمربع
helix	螺旋	لولب ، حافة الاذن الخارجية
hemisphere	地球の半球	نصف الكرة
hemophilia	血友病	المزاج النزفي : نزعة وراثية إلى النزف الدموي
high-pressure	高圧の	ضغط عالي
history	歴史	تاريخ
hollow	うつろな	مُجَـوّف
homogeneity	同種	تجانُس
homosexuality	同性愛	اللواطة
horizontal	水平の	أفقي
hormone	ホルモン	الهرمون
housekeeper	家計を切りもりする人	مدبّرة المنزل
humid	湿気のある	رطب
hybrid	混血種	مُولَّد ، هجين
hydroelectric	水力発電の	كهربيمائي : متعلق بتوليد الكهرباء من القوة المائية
hydrogen	水素	الهيدروجين
hydrostatic	流体静力学の	هيدروستاتي : متعلق بتوازن الموائع وضغطها
hypertension	高血圧（症）	فرط ضغط الدم
hypoglycemia	低血糖（症）	نقص السكر
hypothesis	仮説	الفرضية
idiomatic	慣用語法の	فردي ، اصطلاحي
idiopathic	独特の	فردي ، ذاتي العِلّة : ناشئ عفوياً أو عن عِلّة غامضة
illusion	幻影	وهـم
imagery	像	تخيّلات
to imagine	想像する	يتخيل
imitation	模倣	تقليد
immensity	巨大	ضخامة
imperfection	不完全	نقص ، عيب
inanimate	生命のない	لاحي ، غيرذي حياة
increment	増加	زيادة
indigestible	消化しにくい	عسرُ الهضم
infection	伝染	تلوّث ، عدوى
infestation	浸入	ابتلاء
inflexible	変えられない	صلب ، لا ينثني
infrared	赤外線の	دون الأحمر
ingestion	摂取する	استيعاب
inheritance	相続	ميراث ، أرث
to injure	傷つける	يجرح
to inspect	検査する	يفحص ، يفتش
insulator	絶縁体	العازل
insulin	インシュリン	الأنسولين
intensity	強烈さ	كثافة ، شدة
intercourse	交通関係	اتصال ، جماع
interfere	邪魔をする	يتدخل
intravenously	静脈内に	مُدخَل عن طريق الأوردة
to invade	入り込む	يغزو ، يجتاح

ENGLISH	JAPANESE	ARABIC
inversion	発明	عكس
invisible	見分けにくい	خفي ، غيرمنظور
in vitro	ガラス器内での	خارج الجسم الحي ، في أنبوب اختبار
ionizing	電離すること	تأين ، تحويل إلى أيونات
irregularity	不規則	الشُّذوذيّة
irritability	刺激に敏感なこと	التأثرية قبول الاثارة ، التهيُّجيّة
isotope	アイソトープ	النظير
to jettison	捨てる	يتخلص من ، يطرح
kidney	腎臓	كلية
kingdom	王国	المملكة
laboratory	実験室	مختبر
laser	レーザー	اللازر ، أداة لتضخيم اشعاع الترددات ضمن منطقة النور المنظور
latitude	緯度	خط العرض
layer	層	طبقة
length	長さ	طـول
lens	レンズ	عدسة
to lessen	少くする	يُقَلِّل
levitation	浮揚	سباحة في الهواء
liberation	解放	محرر
lifespan	寿命	عمر : حياة المرء على الأرض
lifetime	生涯	العمر : حياة المرء أو مداها
limb	縁辺	وصل ، طرف
limestone	石灰岩	حجر الكلس
lineaments	特徴	أسارير ، قسمات
lipid	脂質	دهن
lithium	リチウム	الليثيوم
locality	産地	المحلّية : كون الشيء محلياً
logic	論理	منطق ، علم المنطق
lung	肺	رئة
lysine	リジン	حامض أميني
majority	大多数	الأكثرية ، الأغلبية
malfunction	機能不全	قصور
malnutrition	栄養不良	سوء التغذية
mammalia	ほ乳綱	ذوات الأثداء
manganese	マンガン	المغنيز
to manipulate	操作する	يتلاعب بـ ، يؤثر في
manual	手動の	يدوي
to manufacture	製造業者	يصنع
mathematics	数学	رياضي
to maximize	最大化する	يزيد إلى الحد الأعلى
meaningless	無意味な	خلو من المعنى أو المغزى
measurement	測定	القياس
mechanic	機械的な	ميكانيكي ، الصانع اليدوي
medication	薬物処理	معالجة
mercury	水銀	زئبق
metabolism	新陳代謝	مجموع العمليات المتصلة بناء الدوتوبلازما ودثورها
metallic	金属性の	معدني
meteorologist	気象学者	الأرصادي ، العالم بالأرصاد الجوية
microelectronics	マイクロエレクトロニクス	اليكترونيات مجهرية
microscope	顕微鏡	(الميكروسكوب ، المجهر)
microwave	マイクロ波	الموجة الصغرى : موجة كهرطيسية قصيرة جداً
mineral	鉱物	معـدن
to minimize	最小化する	يخفض إلى الحد الأدنى
to modify	改良する	يعدل ، يخفف
module	モジュール	وحدة قياس
mold	鋳型	قالب ، عفن ، تراب وبخاصة ثرى ناعم غني بالمادة العضوية
molecule	分子	الجزيىء
mosquito	蚊	بعوضة
mud	泥	وحل ، طين
mule	らば	بغل
multiple	多数の	مُركّب ، مضاعف ، متعدد
multispectral	多スペクタル感応性の	ذو مجالات متعددة
multitude	多数	متعدد

ENGLISH	JAPANESE	ARABIC
muscle	筋肉	عضلة
myelin	ミリエン	النخاعين
nacelle	つりかご	كنّة المحرك : حجرة مقفلة في طائرة خاصة بالمحرك وقد تفرد أحياناً للملاحين
narrative	物語	قصة ، سرد الأخبار
natural gas	天然ガス	الغاز الطبيعي
nautical	航海の	بحري : متعلق بالبحارة أو السفن
navigation	航行	ابحار ، ملاحة
neon	ネオン	مصباح تفريغ أنبوبي الشكل يكون فيه الغاز ، غاز النيون ، محتوياً على مقدار كبير من النيون
neuter	中性	ليس بالمذكر ولا بالمؤنث ، حيادي
neutral	中性の	محايد
nickel	ニッケル	النيكل ، النكلة : قطعة نقدية قيمتها خمس سنتات
nitric	窒素の	نتريك : محتو على نتروجين خماسي التكافؤ
nitrogen	窒素	النتروجين
nocturnal	夜の	ليلّ ، ناشط في الليل
non-prescription	医者の処方せんなしで買える	وصفة غير طبيّة
normotensive	正常血圧の	(شخص) ذو ضغط دم عادي أو طبيعي
nozzle	管先	الأنف
nuclear	核の	نَوَوي
nylon	ナイロン	النيلون
obesity	肥満	بدانة
obscure	暗い	غامض
observation	観視すること	مراقبة ، ملاحظة
oceanographer	海洋学	الأوقيانوغرافي : العالم بالمحيطات
offshore	沖合の	بعيداً عن الشاطيء
oilshale	油母頁岩	الطين المحتوي على النفط
opaque	不透明体	المعتمة : مادة ملوّنة تستعمل لتعتيم ، جزء من الصورة السلبية ، مبهم
ophthalmologist	眼科医	طبيب العيون
oral	口で行う	متعلق بالفم ، شفهي
organism	有機物	الكائن الحي
origin	起始点	نشوء ، الأصل
ornithologist	鳥類学者	العالم بالطيور
outpost	最先端	مركز أو نقطة الحدود
overactive	あまり活動しすぎる	مفرط النشاط
oversimplification	極度の単純化	تبسيط شديد
overweight	重すぎる	أثقل من الضروري أو المسموح به
oxide	オキシデート	أكسيد
oxygen	酸素	الأكسجين
pain	痛み	ألم
parachute	パラシュート	مظلّة
parasite	寄生するもの	الطُفيلي ، حيوان أو نبات متطفل على حيوان أو نبات آخر
particulates	微粒子	دقائق
pathogenic	病源の	مسبب مرضاً ، ممرض
penicillin	ペニシリン	البنيسيلين : عقار مضاد للجراثيم
penumbra	半影部	شبه الظل
percentage	パーセント	نسبة مئوية
perception	知覚	القدرة على الفهم ، الادراك الحسي
to perch	座る	يحط الطائر
periodically	定期的に	دورياً
peripheral	周辺の	محيطي : متعلق بمحيط ، سطحي ، خارجي
perpendicular	垂直	عمودي
petri dish	シャーレ	صحن زجاجي صغير رقيق ذو غطاء مرن يستعمل بخاصة في المختبرات لزرع البكتيريا
petrochemical	石油化学製品	المادة البتروكيميائية
petroleum	石油	البترول ، النفط
phenomena	事象	واقعة أو حادثة قابلة للوصف والتفسير العلميين ، ظاهرة
phosphate	リン酸塩	الفوسفات
phosphorus	リン	فسفوري
photochemical	光化学物質	كيميائي ضوئي
photon	光子	الفوتون : وحدة الكم الضوئي
photosphere	光球	سطح الشمس النيّر ، كرة ضوئية

ENGLISH	JAPANESE	ARABIC
photosynthesis	光合成の	التخليق أو التركيب الضوئي
photovoltaic	光電池の	كهربائي ضوئي
phylum	門	الشعبة (في تصنيف الحيوان والنبات)
physically	身体上	جسديا
physician	内科医	الطبيب
physics	物理学	الفيزياء
physiology	生理学	الفيسيولوجيا : علم وظائف الأعضاء
pilot	パイロット	القائد ، الدليل
planet	惑星	نجم ، كوكب سيّار
plasmid	プラスミド	بلازما
plywood	合板	الخشب الرقائقي
poison	毒	سُمّ
polarity	極性	القطبية ، الاستقطابية
political	政治に関する	سياسي
pollen	花粉	غبار الطلع ، لقاح
pollutant	汚染物	الملوّن
polymer	ポリマー	البوليمر : مركب كيميائي يُشكل بالتَّبَلْمُر
population	人口	السُّكان
portion	部分	قسم ، جزء
positron	陽電子	البوزترون : جُسيم موجب ذو كتلة تعادل كتلة الالكترون
precarious	不安定な	متقلقل
precaution	用心	احتراس
pregnancy	妊娠	حمل
prematurely	尚早に	ولادة قبل الأوان
prescription	処方せん	وصفة طبّية
prevention	防止	منع
procedure	手続き	البروتوكول ، إجراء
process	プロセス	عملية
prognosis	予後	التكهن
projectile	発射できる	قذيفة
promising	見込みのある	ينتظره مستقبل مرموق
prone	うつぶせの	عرضة بـ ، ميّال أو نزّاع إلى
propane	プロパン	غاز بروبين
protein	蛋白質	البروتين
proton	陽子	البروتون ، جسيم يحمل وحدة من الكهربائية الموجبة ويشكل جزءاً من الذرة
protozoan	原生動物	البَرْزَوي
proximity	近いこと	قرب (في المكان أو الزمان)
pulse rate	脈拍数	معدل النبض
to purify	精化する	يُطهِّر
quantity	量	كمية
quartz	石英	المَرْو ، الكوارتز
to radiate	放射する	يُشِع
radioactive	放射能のある	إشعاعي النشاط
radium	ラディウム	الراديوم : عنصر فلزي اشعاعي النشاط
radon	ラドン	الرادون ، غاز الرادون
rapid	早い	سريع
ray	射出	شعاع
reaction	反応	رد فعل ، تفاعل
reattachment	再逮捕	إعادة وصل
recognition	承認	تمييز ، تعرف
recombinant	遺伝子間組換えの	إعادة مزج
to reconstruct	復元する	يبني أو ينظم من جديد
to recoup	埋めあわせをする	يعوض ، يسترد ، يستعيد
to regenerate	回生させる	يشكل نسيجاً أو عضواً جديداً يحل محل نسيج أو عضو مفقود ، يجدّد
relationship	関係	علاقة ، قرابة
renal	腎臓の	كلوي : ذو علاقة بالكليتين
reproduction	生殖	إنتاج ، تكاثر ، نسخة طبق الأصل
reptile	爬虫類	من الزواحف ، الزاحف
reputation	世評	شهرة ، سمعة
research	研究	بحث ، البحث العلمي
resin	樹脂	الرّاتينج : مادة صمغية تسيل من معظم الأشجار عند قطعها أو جرحها

ENGLISH	JAPANESE	ARABIC
to resist	負けない	يقاوم
respiration	呼吸	تنفّس
responsibility	責任	مسؤولية
responsive	応答的な	سريع الاستجابة ، مستجيب
to restrict	制限する	يحدّد ، يقيّد
results	結果	نتائج
to retard	進行を防げる	يؤخّر ، يعوق
retina	網膜	الشبكيّة ، شبكة العين
to reverse	逆にする	يعكس ، يقلب
revolution	変革	الدوران ، طواف جرم سماوي في مدار
risk	危険	مخاطرة
robot	ロボット	الرّبوط : إنسان أنوماتيكي أوآلي
rocket	ロケット	قنبلة أو قذيفة صاروخية
to ruin	破滅する	يخرّب ، يدمّر
saccharin	サッカリン	السُّكّرين : مركب متبلر أحلى من قصب السكر مئات المرات
salmon	サケ	السّلمون
to scatter	四散させる	يفرّق ، يبعثر
scholar	学者	عالم
science	科学	علم
scurvy	壊血病	الأسقربوط : داء من أعراضه تورّم اللثة ونزف الدم منها
sea level	海面	مستوى سطح البحر
secretion	分泌（液）	إفراز
seismograph	震動記録	المِرجفة : مِرسمة الزلازل
self-generating	自生	توليد ذاتي
self-limiting	自ら制限した	تحديد ذاتي
self-supporting	自給している	كاف نفسه بنفسه
self-sustaining	自給している	معيل نفسه بنفسه
sensory	知覚の	حسي : ذو علاقة بالاحساس
serious	重大な	جدّي
sex-linked	伴性の	ذو علاقة بالجنس
shallow	浅い	ضحل ، قليل العمق
shark	鮫	القرش : سمك مفترس
silicon	ケイ素	السّليكون : مركب سليكوني عضوي
simultaneous	同時の	متزامن ، حادث في وقت واحد
skull	頭骨	جمجمة ، عقل
slide rule	計算尺	المسطرة الحاسبة
smog	スモッグ	الضّبخن : مزيج من ضباب ودخان
smokestack	煙突	مدخنة
to sneeze	くしゃみをする	يعطس
sodium	ナトリウム	الصوديوم
solar	太陽の	شمسي
solidified	凝固、結晶した	متجمّد ، متصلّب
soluble	溶解できる	ذؤوب : قابل للذوبان في سائل
solvent	溶剤	المذيب : مادة مذيبة
sonic	音の	صوتي
sophisticated	洗練された	مغشوش ، متكلّف ، محرّف
source	源	مصدر
spacecraft	宇宙船	السفينة الفضائية
spatial	空間の	فضائي ، مكاني
specimen	標本	عيّنة ، نموذج
spectrometer	分光計	مقياس الطيف
spectroscopy	分光学	المطيافيّة : التحليل الطيفي باستخدام المطياف
sphygmomanometer	血圧計	المضغاط : أداة لقياس ضغط الدم الشرياني بخاصة
spinal	背骨の	فقري ، شوكي
spiral	螺旋形の	لولبي ، حلزوني
stable	安定性のある	إسطبل
statistics	統計学	إحصائي
steam	水蒸気	بخار
steroid	ステロイド	مركب الستيرويد
stimulus	刺激	الحاضر ، المنبّه
strata	層	طبقات ، أطوار
straw	わら	قش
structure	構造	تركيب ، بنية

ENGLISH	JAPANESE	ARABIC
subclass	亜綱	فـرع رئيسي (من طبقة)
sub-genus	亜属	الجنـس (في تصنيف الحيوان أو النبات)
to submerge	水中に入れる	يَغمُر
subphylum	亜門	الأمّمة (في تصنيف الأحياء)
subsonic	亜音速の	دون (أو أقل) من سرعة الصوت
subspecies	亜種	النويع (في منتصف الأحياء)
substance	内容	جوهر ، مادة
substitute	代理	البديل
subtitle	サブタイトル	عنوان فرعي
sulfite	亜硫酸塩	كبريت
sulfuric	硫黄の	كبريتي
sunspot	黒点	كلفة الشمس : احدى كلف الشمس وهي بقع داكنة تبدو بين فترة وأخرى على سطح الشمس
superbly	壮麗に	ببروعـة
surgeon	外科医	الجرّاح : الطبيب الجرّاح
sweetener	甘味料	محلّي
systolic	心収縮の	انقباضي
talon	爪	مخلَب ، إصبع الانسان أو يده
technician	専門技術者	الفني : الاختصاصي بالدقائق التقنية لموضوع أو حرفة ما
telescope	望遠鏡	التلِسكوب
tension	緊張	توتّر
terrestrial	陸上の	أحد سكان الأرض ، أرضي
territory	領域	منطقة ، أقليم
test tube	試験管	أنبوب الاختبار
therapy	療法	مداواة
thermocouple	熱電対	المزدوجة الحرارية
thermometer	温度計	ميزان الحرارة
thrombosis	血栓症	الخثَر : تكوّن الخلطة أو وجودها في الوعاء الدموي
thyrotoxicosis	甲状腺中毒症	ثايروتكسيكوسيس
tomography	断層撮影	الرسم السطحي أو الطبقي (بأشعة إكس)
topaz	トパーズ	التوباز : حجر كريم مختلف الأشكال والألوان
topmost	一番高い	الأعلى
transplant	移殖	ازدراع
treatment	処置	معاملة ، معالجة
tremor	身震い	ارتعاش
trench	掘割り	خندق
tumor	腫れ物	ورم ، ورم خبيث
turbojet	ターボジェット	النفاثة التربينية : طائرة مزودة بمحركات تربينية نفاثة
turbulence	乱流	تمرد ، اضطراب
ulcer	潰瘍	قُرحة
unborn	まだ生まれていない	لم يولد بعد ، مُقبِل
unconsciousness	無意識	اللّا شعور ، اللّا وعي
uncontaminated	汚れていない	غير ملوّث
unconventional	因襲にとらわれない	غير تقليدي
uninhabited	禁じられていない	غير مأهول بالسكان ، غير مسكون
universe	全世界	الكون
unreachable	手の届かない	غير ممكن الوصول اليه
uranium	ウラン	اليورانيوم
urine	尿	بَول
vaccination	予防接種	تلقيح
variant	変種	متنوع
verification	検証	التثبت من ، التحقق من
vertebrate	脊椎動物	الفقاري : حيوان من الفقاريات
vertical	垂直の	عمودي
to vibrate	振動する	يهز ، يذبذب
volcano	火山（口）	بركان
to vomit	吐く	يلفظ ، يتقيأ
watt-hour	ワット時	الواط الساعي
wavelength	波長	الطول الموجي
to weld	溶接する	يلحُم
whale shark	ジンベイザメ	حوت قرشي
to whiten	白くする	يبيّض
windmill	風車	الهيليكوبتر ، الطاحونة الهوائية

ENGLISH	JAPANESE	ARABIC
windshield	風防	حاجب الريح : الحاجب الزجاجية
x-ray	X 線	الأشعة السينية : أشعة إكس
zinc	亜鉛	الزُنك ، الخارصين : عضو فلزي أبيض مزرق
zone	一帯	منطقة ، المنطقة الكروية